One Thing Needful

Mark Weis

Mark Weis
One Thing Needful

Copyright 2017 by Mark Weis

ISBN: 978-1-5211-5673-5

For my sons, Justin and Andrew.

You will always be God's greatest earthly gifts to me.
I was with you when you were born.
I've watched you grow into fine young men
of whom I am immensely proud.

Remember above all else
that the *One Thing Needful* in your lives
is not fame or fortune but the word of God.

Only God can love you more than I do.

-Dad

CONTENTS

A LESSON IN HUMILITY

Luke 14:1-11

Jesus was at a wedding banquet. When He noticed how the guests were choosing the best seats, He told them this parable: "When you are invited by anyone to a wedding feast, do not sit down in the best place, lest one more honorable than you be invited by him; and he who invited you and him come and say to you, 'Give place to this man,' and then you begin with shame to take the lowest place. But when you are invited, go and sit down in the lowest place, so that when he who invited you comes he may say to you, 'Friend, go up higher.' Then you will have glory in the presence of those who sit at the table with you. For whoever exalts himself will be humbled, and he who humbles himself will be exalted,' " Luke 14:8-11.

Luke 14:11 is obviously the core of Christ's lesson on humility. And the lesson is very clear: Exalt yourself, be humbled. Humble yourself, be exalted. And what's so striking about this lesson is the inevitability of the consequences.

Notice that Jesus did not say "might be" or "could be" or "should be" but "will be." "Whoever exalts himself *will* be humbled, and he who humbles himself *will* be exalted." We see this principle illustrated every day. The criminal who thought he'd never be caught. The politician who thought he was above the law. The dictator who thought he was invincible.

But if the consequences of pride are sobering, the consequences of humility are comforting. The Bible states: "God opposes the proud but gives grace to the humble," James 4:6. When we humble ourselves before God; when we acknowledge our sins and failings; when we wait for Him to exalt us—in terms of Christ's parable to say, "Friend, go up higher"—God will lift us up. It is inevitable, as Jesus said: "He who humbles himself will be exalted."

I've often wondered why God allowed me to go through difficult circumstances in life, some of which proved very humbling. Losses of various kinds. Nagging injuries. Moving from a beautiful home in the suburbs to a one-bedroom apartment on the third floor of an apartment complex.

But this is what I've learned: If God allows me to go through trying circumstances, it is only because He loves me and wants to strip away my false pretenses and foolish pride. He wants me to learn anew the all-important lesson of humility so that I trust in Him instead of myself. This was no doubt the reason Simon Peter wrote to the struggling Christians of Asia Minor: "Humble yourselves, therefore, under God's mighty hand, that He may lift you up in due time. Cast all your anxiety on Him because He cares for you." 1 Peter 5:6-7.

We may wonder at times, "Why should Christians need a lesson in humility? We aren't prideful Pharisees." No, by the grace of God we are not. We are children of God led by the Spirit of God. Yet, in this life we still retain the old sinful nature. And it's that old sinful nature that constantly prods us to be proud of our humility.

On the night in which Jesus instituted His Holy Supper, He—God Himself—got down on His hands and knees and washed the filthy feet of His disciples. When finished, He said, "Do you understand what I have done for you? You call Me 'Teacher' and 'Lord,' and rightly so, for that is what I am. Now that I, your Lord and Teacher have washed your feet, you should also wash one another's feet. I have set you an example that you should do as I have done for you," John 13:12-15.

His example was selfless humility. And that is the lesson.

THE ARMOR OF GOD

Ephesians 6:10-17

"Know your enemy." This has been sound military strategy for millennia. It is sound spiritual strategy too. Paul wrote in Ephesians 6:12, "For our struggle is not against flesh and blood, but against the rulers, against the authorities, against the powers of this dark world, and against spiritual forces of evil in the heavenly realms."

The devil is not a conventional enemy and cannot be hurt by conventional weapons of war—flame-throwers, bunker-busters, and nuclear missiles. He is a powerful fallen angel of immense strength and cunning. Having studied human nature for thousands of years, he knows human desires and weaknesses and how to exploit them. Using our own strength, we have no chance of defeating the devil. Conversely, when we are "strong in the Lord and in His mighty power," Ephesians 6:10, the devil has no chance of defeating us. We are strong in the Lord when we "put on the armor of God."

Paul was a Roman citizen and familiar with Roman soldiers and their armor. In fact, he wrote Ephesians while in a Roman prison. He could no doubt see the armor of the guards while describing the armor of God. And when Paul listed God's armor, he did so in the exact order in which a Roman legionnaire put his armor on.

"Stand firm then, with the belt of truth buckled around your waist," Ephesians 6:14. A Roman soldier put his belt on first because it prevented his tunic from getting in the way during the heat of battle. The belt also kept his breastplate in place, and held such weapons as a sword and dagger. So the belt was very important to the soldier.

The truth of Scripture is very important to the Christian. "Your word is truth," Jesus said in John 17:17. This means that everything God tells us in His word is absolutely true and utterly reliable. The devil is a liar and cannot abide or withstand God's truth.

"With the breastplate of righteousness in place," Ephesians 6:14. The breastplate covered the vital organs in the chest, especially the heart. In a similar way, the righteousness of Jesus Christ covers, calms, and saves us. When the devil accuses us—the name "devil" means "accuser"—we find refuge in such comforting Bible passages as "There is now no condemnation for those who are in Christ Jesus," Romans 8:1; and "God made Him who had no sin to be sin for us, so that in Him we might become the righteousness of God," 2 Corinthians 5:21; and "The blood of Jesus Christ, His Son, cleanses us from all sin," 1 John 1:7.

"And with your feet fitted with the readiness that comes from the gospel of peace," Ephesians 6:15. The shoes of a Roman soldier were called *caligae*. Thick-soled and hob-nailed, the *caligae* protected the feet during long marches and provided traction on slippery terrain. It is

13

the gospel of peace—peace with God through our Lord Jesus Christ—that keeps us moving forward and gives us 'traction' during the battles in our lives. Jesus said in John 14:27, "Peace I leave with you. My peace I give you. I do not give to you as the world gives. Do not let your hearts be troubled and do not be afraid."

"In addition to all this, take up the shield of faith, with which you can extinguish all the flaming arrows of the evil one," Ephesians 6:16. The shield of a Roman legionnaire was about four feet long and curved to protect the body. Our faith in Jesus Christ shields us from the attacks and accusations of the devil. And faith, as Scripture explains, is simply taking God at His word.

If God says He will save you, He will. If God says He will deliver you from trouble, He will. If God says He will forgive you when you turn to Him in faith and repentance, He will. If God says He will provide for your daily needs despite the daily calls from bill collectors, He will.

It is faith in God's faithfulness that acts like a shield, snuffing out all the flaming arrows—doubt, fear, frustration, despair, guilt—of the evil one. Simon Peter wrote in his First Epistle: "Be self-controlled and alert. Your enemy the devil prowls around like a roaring lion looking for someone to devour. Resist him, standing firm in the faith," 1 Peter 5:8.

"Take the helmet of salvation," Ephesians 6:17. The helmet protected the soldier's head. God's helmet of salvation protects the Christian's mind. It focuses our

thoughts "on things above," Colossians 3:2, helping to protect us from temptation and the lusts and pleasures of this world. It also calms our excessive anxiety, reminding us "that if God is for us, who can be against us? He who did not spare His own Son, but gave Him up for us all—how will He not also, along with Him, graciously give us all things?" Romans 8:31-32.

"And the sword of the Spirit, which is the word of God," Ephesians 6:17. The writer of Hebrews said, "For the word of God is living and active. Sharper than any doubled-edged sword, it penetrates even to dividing soul and spirit, joints and marrow; it judges the thoughts and attitudes of the heart," Hebrews 4:12. Jesus wielded the word of God like a sword when tempted by the devil in the wilderness. Again and again the Savior said, "It is written. It is written. It is written."

Before the word of God, the devil has no choice but to flee in defeat. And so the sword of the Spirit, the word of God, equips us for life; and enables us to cut down all the lies, all the doubts, all the temptations of the devil. As Martin Luther wrote in his great Reformation hymn: "Though devils all the world should fill, all eager to devour us; we tremble not, we fear no ill, they shall not overpower us. This world's prince may still scowl fierce as he will. He can harm us none. He's judged; the deed is done. One little word can fell him."

BEHOLD YOUR KING

Matthew 21:1-11

Palm Sunday is a joyful occasion. And this God intended. Centuries before the birth of Christ, God said through the prophet Zechariah: "Rejoice greatly, O Daughter of Zion! Shout, Daughter of Jerusalem! See, your King comes to you, righteous and having salvation, gentle and riding on a donkey, on a colt, the foal of a donkey," Zechariah 9:9.

But what makes Palm Sunday so joyful? If the multitudes that first Palm Sunday had known the answer, they would not have shouted "hosanna" on Sunday and "crucify" on Friday. And sadly, even the Lord's disciples failed to recognize the true significance of this event—and would not, according to John 12:16, until after Jesus was glorified. What is it about Christ's entry into Jerusalem on Palm Sunday that should move us to greatly rejoice?

"Say to the Daughter of Zion, 'See…'" Matthew 21:5. The Greek word translated "see" means to pay close attention. What did God want us to see when Jesus rode a donkey into Jerusalem. "See, your King comes to you." How remarkable is this? Would the president of the United States come to you? Would a local congressman return a single phone call? Yet, God's entire plan of salvation could be summarized in these six words: "See, your King comes to you."

And what these words say collectively to the Daughter of Zion they also say to us as individuals. Regardless of who you are, what you've done, where you've been, what burdens you may be carrying, your King, Jesus Christ, came to redeem you.

Unlike earthly kings, Jesus is the gentle King. And what makes His gentleness all the more remarkable is that He is the eternal Son of God, exercising all power in heaven and on earth. Jesus could have ridden into Jerusalem on Palm Sunday astride a prancing white stallion and surrounded by all the host of heaven. Instead, He entered Jerusalem on a lowly donkey.

Is there really a need to discuss how different King Jesus is from earthly kings, rulers, dictators, and elected officials? We read about their self-interest and abuses of power daily. The Greek word translated as "gentle" in Matthew 21:5 is the very same word Jesus used in His precious invitation: "Come to Me, all of you who are weary and burdened, and I will give you rest. Take My yoke upon you and learn from Me, for I am *gentle* and humble in heart, and you will find rest for your souls," Matthew 11:28-29.

And finally, King Jesus is the only king who keeps His word. How does this compare with earthly rulers? Notice what Matthew wrote in verse 4: "This took place to fulfill what was spoken through the prophet." It is truly amazing and comforting to realize that everything Jesus did for us— from riding into Jerusalem on Palm Sunday to dying on the cross on Good Friday—He did to fulfill God's promises of salvation and to demonstrate the utter reliability of the Holy Scriptures.

BE OPENED!

Mark 7:31-37

Mark 7:33 states, "He put His fingers into the man's ears." A finger in the ear is a recognizable gesture. For us it usually means, "Huh? I didn't hear that. Could you repeat it? I don't understand. Maybe I need to clean my ears out." Only, we cannot clean out our "spiritual" ears with our own fingers. This type of opening and cleaning requires the finger of almighty God.

You believe in God. You believe that Jesus Christ is your Lord and Savior, and that His death on the cross atoned for all your sins. You believe that manna fell from heaven; that Mary Magdalene clasped the feet of the risen Jesus; that the walls of Jericho crumbled when seven priests sounded seven trumpets for the seventh time. But you did not choose to believe any of these Bible truths on your own. You believe because the Lord Jesus put His fingers into your ears and said, "*Ephphatha!* Be opened!"

Jesus not only opened the deaf-mute's ears, He also loosed the man's tongue. And He has done the same for us—for which reason we say with the Psalmist: "O Lord, open my lips, and my mouth shall show forth Your praise," Psalm 51:15. It is through His word that God creates the miracle of faith; and it is through the miracle of faith that God opens our mouths to proclaim His word. The two are inseparable.

Paul wrote in Romans 1:16, "For I am not ashamed of the gospel of Christ, for it is the power of God for the salvation of everyone who believes." The Greek word translated as power in this verse, DUNAMIS, is the source of our English word *dynamite*. The gospel is God's dynamite. And therefore, the power to save and effect change lies in the word of God, not in the listener or proclaimer. The deaf-mute was empowered to hear by the very word he could not hear: "*Ephphatha!* Be opened!"

When you and I are concerned about the faith of another person, the best thing we can do is to do what the friends of the deaf-mute did for him. They brought the man to Jesus and let Him work the miracle. This does not mean hounding anyone with religious pamphlets. It means gently and lovingly sharing Christ at each opportunity. It means sending a note with a Bible verse. It means personally explaining what God in Christ has done for you.

Imagine how difficult the deaf-mute's life was before Jesus came into it. The man's disability would have prevented him from getting a job. Without a job he would have been entirely dependent on others. Without others to depend on, he would have been forced to beg. But Jesus Christ changed all that. And how did the former deaf-mute respond? He couldn't stay quiet. He couldn't stop praising God, speaking words clearly with his own mouth, and hearing words for the first time with his own ears.

How has your life changed with Jesus in it—knowing that He suffered and died to save you; knowing that He cares eternally about you and sighs deeply at your hurts and tears; knowing that He is always near you, always listening to you, always interceding for you; knowing that Jesus led you away from the crowd and made you one of His own; knowing that you would never have known Jesus as Savior had He not opened your ears, mouth, heart, and life with His "*Ephphatha!* Be opened!"?

If at times the word of God seems too mundane, boring, or predictable for us; if at times our worship seems joyless or a waste of a Sunday morning; perhaps we've forgotten what it is like to be spiritually dead, deaf, and mute. Perhaps we've taken for granted our ears and tongues, our hearing and speaking, our faith and confession.

THE BREAD OF LIFE

John 6:24-35

John 6 opens with the miraculous feeding of the five thousand. We all know the details—how Jesus fed the multitudes with only five small barley loaves and two small fish; and afterwards, how the disciples gathered twelve basketfuls of leftovers.

Yet, who told Jesus the multitudes were hungry? Were the crowds waving cardboard signs which read: HUNGRY. WILL WORK FOR FOOD? No. According to John 6:5-6, Jesus Himself was the one who first mentioned food: "When Jesus looked up and saw a great crowd coming toward Him, He said to Philip, 'Where shall we buy food for these people to eat?' He said this only to test him, for He already had in mind what He was going to do."

In other words, Jesus intended to feed the crowds before they knew they were hungry; before He heard the first grumbling stomach or the first crying infant. In His divine hands—the same hands that shaped the universe and were later nailed to the cross—having only five loaves of bread and two small fish did not matter. Jesus still fed the multitudes liberally, to the point of leftovers. How many leftovers did you and I place into Tupperware containers last night or toss into the trash?

Shame on us when we, as Christians, behave like the unbelieving world, running about in a blind panic and saying, "What shall we eat? What shall we drink? What shall we wear?"—as if God didn't know our needs and had no desire to supply them. And shame on us even more when we credit ourselves for daily bread instead of God. "But I'm the one who goes to work; God doesn't. The corporate comptroller signs my paycheck; God doesn't. The supermarket supplies my groceries; God doesn't." Nonsense! Who makes the sun shine and the rain fall? Who makes the seeds germinate and the plants grow to feed the livestock, so that we have food on our tables? Not the supermarket. God.

Of course, there is a hunger far greater than physical hunger, and it can only be satisfied by a far greater food—not an earthly food, but a heavenly food; the type of food of which Jesus spoke in John 6:35, "I am the bread of life;" and in 6:41, "I am the bread that came down from heaven;" and in 6:51, "I am the living bread that came down from heaven."

Everyone recognizes physical hunger: the growling stomach, the feeling of emptiness, the hunger pangs. But apart from the Holy Spirit, no one can recognize the nature, cause, or cure of spiritual hunger, even when experiencing its symptoms.

The symptoms often include feelings of loneliness, purposelessness, and emptiness. Knowing that something is missing from life, but not knowing what. Searching for happiness in wealth and possessions, but never finding it.

Longing for answers to the nagging questions that have plagued humanity since the Fall into Sin: Who am I? Why am I here? What's my purpose? What is the meaning of life? What happens to me when I die?

And when people don't know the answers; when they fail to recognize their spiritual hunger and their need for Jesus, the Bread of Life; they often turn to harmful things—drugs, alcohol, the fad diets and happy meals of human philosophies. Isn't alcoholism the ongoing attempt to "fill up on happiness" from a bottle? Isn't drug abuse the ongoing attempt to "fill up on happiness" by ingesting pills or injecting needles or inhaling powder.

Sadly, people who pursue these things are never satisfied. Why? Because no earthly food can satisfy spiritual hunger. Only God can fill the God-sized hole in each human heart. Only Jesus Christ, the Bread of Life, can satisfy our emptiness. Jesus said, "I am the bread of life. He who comes to Me will never go hungry, and he who believes in Me will never be thirsty."

The instant anyone turns to Christ, that deeper hunger, our spiritual hunger, goes away—forever.

THE RIGHT FOUNDATION

Matthew 7:24-27

We seldom think about the foundation of a house. However, the foundation is really the most important part of a house, because every other component of the house depends on its foundation: floors, walls, ceiling, and roof. A foundation not only holds a house up; it holds a house firmly in place. Which part of a house is built first? Which part bears the entire weight? Which part provides underlying strength and stability? The foundation.

Obviously, everything depends upon having the right foundation. And if this is true of your house, it is even truer of your life. In Matthew 7:24-27 Jesus teaches us the importance of building our lives on the right foundation; and that right foundation is the eternal, immovable, rock-solid foundation of His word.

Everyone is a Builder
Each of us is a builder. Each of us builds our life on something. And we don't just build our own foundation. As parents, grandparents, siblings, and friends, we help build the lives of others. From the biblical perspective, there are but two types of building materials: the word of God, and then everything else.

Does it matter which building material we use? Some will tell you that it doesn't matter. They say, "Believe in

Jesus or believe in yourself. Believe in Christ or believe in Buddha. Different religions are just different avenues to the same divine place."

True? Absolutely not. And if the words of Jesus in John 14:6 aren't enough—Jesus said, "I am the way and the truth and the life. No one comes to the Father except through Me"—consider the outcome of the wise and foolish builders in our text. The two houses in the parable faced the same storm, but only one house stood while the other completely collapsed. What made the difference? Not the house, builder, or storm, but rather having the right foundation.

Preparing for Storms

Storms are inevitable in life. Notice the identical language Jesus used in verses 25 and 27: "And the rain descended, the floods came, and the winds blew." Jesus did not mention a thirty-percent chance of rain or the possibility of afternoon thunderstorms. He said that storms *will* come. The time to prepare for them is now.

In the *Parable of the Wise and Foolish Builders*, the only house that survived the storm "was founded on the rock," Matthew 7:25. But an even more literal translation of this verse is that the house "had been founded on the rock;" that is, the foundation of that house, that life, had been constructed long before the storm arrived.

In 1992, Hurricane Andrew destroyed thousands of homes in southern Florida. Yet, in an area where the wreckage resembled a war zone, one house remained standing, still firmly anchored to its foundation. When a reporter asked the homeowner why his house had survived, he replied, "I built this house myself. I also built it according to the Florida State Building Code. When the code called for 2x6 roof trusses, I used 2x6 roof trusses. I was told that a house built according to code could withstand a hurricane. And it did."

Build the foundation of your life on Jesus Christ and His word, and you will never be disappointed. His building code comes with a guarantee. "So this is what the Sovereign LORD says: 'See, I lay a stone in Zion, a tested stone, a precious cornerstone for a sure foundation; the one who trusts in Him (Christ) will never be dismayed."

CHANGE

Psalm 27

The first six verses of Psalm 27 are brimming with confidence. "The LORD is my light and my salvation," says David, "whom shall I fear?" However, in verse 7, the tone changes from triumph to uncertainty. David writes "answer me," verse 7; "do not hide Your face" and "do not reject or forsake me," verse 9; and "I had fainted," verse 13.

This abrupt change has led some commentators to conclude that David wrote Psalm 27 in two stages, each stage separated by years. Did he? Possibly. But perhaps there is a simpler explanation. Real life can change that abruptly, that quickly. Haven't we all experienced at least one incident, one phone call, one knock on the door, one consultation with a doctor, that instantly changed our lives?

Change is a part of life, and it impacts all of us. Yet, one of the key messages of Psalm 27 is that we never face change alone. God is always with us. Thirteen times in Psalm 27 David uses the Hebrew name YAVEH for God, the source of our English *Jehovah*. This name, YAVEH, is not a noun or pronoun, but a verb. It means, "I AM."

Though we often imagine God has forsaken us, His very name declares the opposite: "I AM." In Matthew 28:20 Jesus promises, "Surely, I am with you always, to the very end of the age." In Hebrews 13 God declares, "Never will I leave you; never will I forsake you."

Put the principle into practice. When you lose a job, then and there the Lord is saying, "Don't lose hope. I AM with you." When you are struggling to repair a troubled marriage, then and there the Lord is saying, "Don't give up. I AM with you." When you receive a bad report from your doctor and you're frightened, then and there the Lord is saying, "Don't be afraid. I AM with you."

This great name for God, "I AM," is not only the guarantee of God's eternal presence, but also the guarantee of His changelessness. "I the LORD do not change," says God in Malachi 3:6. "Jesus Christ is the same yesterday and today and forever," states Hebrews 13:8. Can you think of anything more comforting, uplifting, or inspiring than the promise of an UNCHANGING GOD in a constantly changing world?

When confronted by change, don't think God Himself is changing. God cannot change. He loves you in the good times, and He still loves you in the bad times. He is never for you one day and against you the next day. He never grows sleepy, bored, or irritable; rather, according to Scripture, He loves you with an everlasting love and enfolds you in an everlasting embrace. "O give thanks to the LORD for He is good. His love endures *forever*," Psalm 136.

GREAT FAITH

Matthew 15:21-28

Jesus had much to say about faith in God—and the lack of it. He not only denounced religious leaders and even entire cities for their stubborn refusal to believe; He also admonished His own disciples for littleness of faith.

But the Gospels also record two instances when Jesus commended individuals for having great faith. One of these was the Canaanite woman in Matthew 15; a Gentile to whom Jesus said, "Woman, you have great faith." What made her faith a great faith?

She Brought Her Problems to Jesus

The Canaanite woman's daughter was being cruelly tormented by a demon. We can imagine this mother's pain, because nothing hurts a parent more than a hurting child. But where did she turn for help? To Jesus Christ. Why? Because her faith recognized Jesus to be the Son of God and long-awaited Savior. "Lord, Son of David," she addressed Him. "Help me," she pleaded, kneeling before Him in worship.

Bringing problems to Jesus may not seem like an attribute of great faith, but it is. Too often we turn to Jesus last, if at all. But faith is only as great as its object. It should be painfully obvious that faith based on human beings has human limitations; and that faith placed in temporal items is a temporary faith. Not so with faith based on God. The Canaanite woman brought her problem to Jesus, knowing that only Jesus could help.

She Came in Humility

The Canaanite woman's great faith led her to Jesus for help, but it did not presume to tell Jesus how to help. The woman simply stated her need, and then relied upon Christ's mercy. She did not say, "Jesus, come to my house right now." She did not say, "Jesus, I expect my problem to be solved by noon tomorrow." She did not even ask Jesus to heal her daughter.

What did she say? "Lord, Son of David, have mercy on me. My daughter is suffering terribly from demon-possession," verse 22; and then subsequently in verse 25, a three-word prayer: "Lord, help me." She gave her problem to Jesus, humbly trusting in Him to act at the right time and in the right way. She refused to give up.

By its very nature, faith is forward-looking. One of the characteristics of great faith is that it keeps moving forward. It refuses to give up or shrink back. We see this beautifully exemplified in the Canaanite woman. Nothing stopped her—not the silence of Jesus; not the irritation of the disciples or stares of the crowd; not Christ's reference to being sent "only to the lost sheep of Israel."

When Jesus and His disciples kept walking away, this woman apparently ran ahead, then knelt before Jesus in the middle of the road; knelt so that Jesus had to stop. And even when Jesus offered a final obstacle, saying, "It is not right to toss the children's bread to the dogs," the woman refused to give up. Instead she replied, "Yes, Lord, but even the dogs eat the crumbs that fall from their masters' table." And precisely then she heard Jesus say, "Woman, you have great faith."

And our faith? Do we have this same persistence; the persistence of a Jacob who wrestled with God and said, 'I will not let You go until You bless me?' Do we have the faith of that Canaanite woman; a faith that laid hold of the promises of God and then laid down in the middle of the road, waiting for Jesus to stop? Did the Canaanite woman know something we don't know? Did she possess a personal strength we don't possess?

No. The reality is, her great faith had nothing to do with who she was and everything to do with who God is. She came to Jesus for help, *because she knew who Jesus was*. She trusted in Jesus to do the right thing at the right time, *because she knew who Jesus was*. She refused to give up on Jesus, *because she knew who Jesus was*—knew that He would never give up on her.

The more we know about Jesus, the greater our faith. For good reason Scripture declares: "Consequently, faith comes from hearing the message, and the message is heard through the word of Christ," Roman 10:17.

CONQUERING WORRY

Matthew 6:25-34

Worry is from the Old English word *wyrgan* and originally meant "to strangle." The word's origin is fitting. Worry can literally choke the life out of a worrier. Today there is conclusive scientific evidence that worry is harmful to health. It has been linked to heart and kidney disease, high blood pressure, stroke, cancer, and even arthritis. "Worried sick" is not merely an expression; it is a medical condition. How can worry be conquered? Through the almighty word of God.

Don't Worry

"Do not worry." If a mere man were speaking these words, they would be hollow and meaningless. But the words are God's, the Creator of heaven and earth. And He is the one telling you not to worry. Jesus said in Matthew 6, "Therefore I tell you, do not worry." In the original language this sentence is more literally, "do not begin to worry." When worry appears, squash it. When worry starts, stop it. When worry moves in, evict it. God has not called you to a life of worry, but to a life of joy and peace; as Jesus said in John 10:10, "I have come that they may have life, and have it to the full."

Worrying is Useless

In His *Sermon on the Mount* Jesus asked, "Who of you by worrying can had a single cubit to his height?" Matthew

6:27. The last time you worried, did you make yourself taller? Did you have to buy a new wardrobe or suddenly crouch when passing through doorways? Of course not. Worrying is useless. It won't add a millimeter to your height or a second to your life. "Since you cannot do this very little thing," Jesus said in Luke 12:26, "why do you worry about the rest?" The instant you and I recognize our own inabilities and weaknesses, we open our lives to the limitless possibilities of God's almighty strength.

Give Your Worries to God

I once had a German Shepherd named Maggie. Maggie would gnaw and chew on a bone until her gums bled. When I tried to take the bone away, Maggie would growl at me. This is a realistic portrait of worry. When we worry, we gnaw and chew on our problems, refusing to let them go despite the pain and emotional bleeding our worrying may be causing us. Why do this? God wants us to give all our worries to Him.

Paul wrote in Philippians 4:6-7, "Do not be anxious about anything, but in everything, by prayer and petition, with thanksgiving, present your requests to God. And the peace of God, which transcends all understanding, will guard your hearts and minds in Christ Jesus." When we give our worries to God and leave them with God, we will obtain that transcendent peace of God. The hymnist was right: "Oh, what peace we often forfeit. Oh, what needless pain we bear. All because we do not carry everything to God in prayer."

God Cares

At times our worry stems from a lack of trust in God's love and providence. This is a hard thing for Christians to admit, but it is nonetheless true. Jesus Himself attributed big worries to little faith, saying in Matthew 6: "And why do you worry about clothes? See how the lilies of the field grow. They do not labor or spin. Yet I tell you that not even Solomon in all his splendor was dressed like one of these. If that if how God clothes the grass of the field, which is here today and tomorrow is thrown into the fire, will He not much more clothe you, O you of little faith?"

The key then to worrying less is to trust God more. And the key to trusting God more is to spend more time reading, hearing, and studying His holy word.

The apostle Peter wrote in his First Epistle, "Humble yourselves, therefore, under God's mighty hand, that He may lift you up in due time. Cast all your anxiety on Him because He cares for you."

God is Your Father

"Your Father knows…" Jesus said when discussing worry in the *Sermon on the Mount.* God is our heavenly Father. And as our Father, He will always provide for us; always guide, defend, and protect us; always give us what we truly need—not what we may mistakenly want.

So, stop worrying. Father knows best.

JUST BELIEVE

Mark 5:21-24, 35-43

Jesus said, "In this world you will have trouble," John 16:33. The truthfulness of His words is reflected not only in our personal lives but in the daily news. The question is not *if* we will face trouble, but how we will endure and overcome trouble.

Unfortunately, the human approach to trouble never rises above a locker room pep-talk: "Hang in there. Try not to worry. Things will work out. When the going gets tough, the tough get going." And of course the naïve philosophy of Scarlet O'Hara: "Tomorrow will be another day." Can you imagine offering this advice to a parent who has lost a child, like the synagogue ruler Jairus in Mark 5?

The Bible's approach to trouble is vastly different. The Bible does not say "Things will work out," but rather "In everything *God* works for the good of those who love Him," Romans 8:28. The Bible does not say "Be strong," but rather "Be strong in the Lord and in *His* mighty power," Ephesians 6:10. The Bible does not say to look inward but upward: "I lift up my eyes to the hills—where does my help come from? My help comes from the LORD, the Maker of heaven and earth," Psalm 121:1-2.

In fact, regardless of the type and size of the trouble, the Bible's advice is unflinchingly the same: Trust God. And where is this better illustrated than in the heartwarming words of Jesus to Jairus: "Don't be afraid; just believe," Mark 5:36. In the original Greek, the words "just believe" are written in the present tense, meaning "go on believing" and "never stop believing."

"Don't be afraid; just believe." It's a wondrously simple message, isn't it? There are no complexities, no limitations, and no situations to which this message does not apply, from the first day of school to the last day of life. The context of Jesus' words was not pretend-life but real-life, not a theological dissertation but a desperate father and a dead twelve-year-old girl.

By the grace of God, Jairus did go on believing in Jesus. He continued to believe when messengers arrived with the news: "Your daughter is dead. Why bother the teacher anymore?" Mark 5:35. He continued to believe during the sad walk home. He continued to believe when he saw the mourners and heard the wailing; and when the mourners ridiculed Jesus for saying "the child is not dead but asleep," Mark 5:39. He continued to believe—this must have been the hardest moment—when staring at the lifeless body of his little girl.

And the result of trusting Jesus? Jesus took the dead child's hand and said to her, " *'Talitha, koum!'* (which means, 'Little girl, I say to you, get up!'). Immediately the girl stood up and walked around," Mark 5:41. The point is, trusting Jesus, even amid the worst of troubles, will never end in disappointment.

Today, Jesus is saying the same words to you: "Don't be afraid; just believe." Believe in Me to do the right thing—not what you consider best but what I know is best. Believe in Me to deliver you at the right time, in the right way. Believe in Me to supply you with the strength and wisdom and perseverance you need in your time of trouble. Believe that I am exactly the Savior I profess to be; the Savior who loved you enough to die for you.

"In this world you will have trouble," said Jesus. But how does the verse go on? "Take heart! I have overcome the world."

DON'T JUST STAND THERE

Ephesians 1:15-23

Apart from Christ, there is no true hope. Paul wrote in Ephesians 2:12, "Remember that at that time you were separate from Christ, excluded from citizenship in Israel and foreigners to the covenants of the promise, without hope and without God in the world."

However, at times, even Christians feel hopeless. We are not expressing hope when we make comments like "I don't expect anything good to happen to me. It never does." Or, "I don't know if I can endure this burden another day." Or, "I don't know if God will deliver me from this problem." Yes, we do know. But as Paul prayed, when feeling hopeless we simply need to know God better.

Whatever our personal circumstances, whether waiting for the results of a medical test or lying in a hospital bed; whether mourning the death of a loved one or facing death ourselves; we still have every reason to hope, because true hope is that to which God has called us.

God has said, "Never will I leave you; never will I forsake you," Hebrews 13:5. And again, "He who began a good work in you will carry it on to completion until the day of Christ Jesus," Philippians 1:6. Knowing who God is, and what He has done for us in Jesus Christ, how can we just stand there in hopelessness?

Paul also prayed that his Christian readers would better know their true inheritance—the heavenly Father's real estate which Jesus described in John 14 when referring to His ascension. He said, "In my Father's house are many rooms; if it were not so, I would have told you. I am going there to prepare a place for you."

As Christians, we already own this heavenly inheritance. The "for this reason" of Ephesians 1:15 refers back to all the blessings Paul describes in the first fourteen verses of the chapter. "Praise be to the God and Father of our Lord Jesus Christ, who has blessed us in the heavenly realms with every spiritual blessing in Christ," Ephesians 1:3. He "chose us" in Christ, verse 4. He "predestined us to be adopted as sons" through Christ, verse 5. He "redeemed us" through the blood of Christ, verse 7. He "included" us in and with Christ, verse 13.

No matter what we lose in life, how can that loss even be compared to our eternal inheritance in Christ? How can we just stand there, claiming, "God doesn't love me," or "God doesn't give me anything?" He's given us everything in Jesus Christ both for this life and the next.

When we face difficulties, we are always tempted to think, "God isn't helping. God isn't doing enough." Actually, He is doing more than we can even imagine. This is why Paul prayed that his Christian readers would better know how God is working in their daily lives; and not just working, but exerting the very same almighty power which He "exerted in Christ when He raised Him from the dead and seated Him at His right hand in the heavenly realms," Ephesians 1:19-20.

What if we lived our lives in view of that power? What if we approached our marriages and ministries and problems in view of that power? Would we ever just stand there again?

DO NOT FEAR

Isaiah 41:10-13

Such phrases as "Do not fear" and "Do not be afraid" occur more than three-hundred and twenty-five times in the Bible. Is God trying to tell us something?

Take Your Fears to God in Prayer.
If you are afraid today, take your fears to God in prayer. Say, "God, I'm afraid of losing my job. I'm afraid of this illness. I'm afraid I won't have the strength to overcome temptation." Articulating your fears to God in prayer will not only help you distinguish between real fears and imaginary ones; it will bring you the peace of heart and mind that only God can give.

The apostle Paul wrote, "Do not be anxious about anything, but in everything, by prayer and petition, with thanksgiving, present your requests to God. And the peace of God, which transcends all understanding, will guard your hearts and your minds in Christ Jesus," Philippians 4:6-7.

God Does not Want You to be Afraid.
Paul wrote to Timothy, "For God did not give us a spirit of timidity, but a spirit of power, of love, and of self-discipline," 2 Timothy 1:7. When we read the Bible carefully, we find God telling us not to fear anything, from the simplest task to the most daunting endeavor.

When Abraham faced the impossibility of fathering a child in his old age, God said, "Do not be afraid, Abram. I am your shield, your very great reward," Genesis 15:1. When the Israelites were trapped at the Red Sea, with Pharaoh's army in feverish pursuit, Moses said, "Do not be afraid. Stand firm and you will see the deliverance the LORD will bring you today," Exodus 14:13.

When Jesus taught His disciples not to worry about the basic necessities of life—food, drink, clothing—He said, "Do not fear, little flock, for your Father has been pleased to give you the kingdom," Luke 12:32. When the daughter of Jairus died, even then Jesus told the grieving parents, "Don't be afraid; just believe, and she will be healed," Luke 8:50.

God is with You

In times of trouble we often wonder if God really is with us. But His solemn promise is this: "Do not fear; for I am with you," Isaiah 41:10. And this: "Never will I leave you; never will I forsake you," Hebrews 13:5. And this: "Surely I am with you always, to the very end of the age," Matthew 28:20.

God is not a temporary helper. He does not arrive for the good times and depart in the bad. If almighty God is with you, whom should you fear? A petty dictator in North Korea? A pesky problem at the office?

God is Your God.

"For I am your God," He said in Isaiah 41:10. And how did God become your God? By choice, not by accident. Because He wanted you, not because He was obligated to you. Because He was willing to sacrifice His own Son, Jesus Christ, to redeem you from your sins.

And if God the Father was willing to sacrifice His only Son for you, will He withhold any other blessing from your life? No. Each time you feel fear creeping into your life, place it into the great equation of Romans 8: "What, then, shall we say in response to this? If God is for us, who can be against us?"

God will Strengthen You and Give You Victory.
You have His word on it. "I will strengthen you and help you; I will uphold you with My righteous right hand. All who rage against you will surely be ashamed and disgraced; those who oppose you will be as nothing and perish. Though you search for your enemies, you will not find them. Those who wage war against you will be as nothing at all," Isaiah 41:10-12.

When we say, "I can't fix this problem;" or "I can't endure this burden;" or "I can't take this situation any longer"—there is entirely too much "I" and too little God. When did He ask us to find strength within ourselves? He didn't. Instead, He has told us to find strength in Him.

Today, open your Bible, turn to Isaiah 41:10-13, and in the margin write: "By the grace of God, today is the day I stopped being afraid."

EASTER CHANGED EVERYTHING

Matthew 28:1-10

"Jesus lives!" As Christians, we know this to be true. The Gospels and Epistles proclaim the resurrection of Jesus so loudly and so often that to deny the resurrection is to call God Himself a bold-faced liar. But having the facts of Easter is not the same as applying Easter.

At least three times—Matthew 16:21; 17:23; and 20:19—Jesus promised His disciples that He would rise from the dead on the third day. Yet, when the first Easter dawned, the first disciples were not expecting a risen Lord but mourning a dead Savior.

Women who visited the garden tomb worried about rolling away the stone. Mary Magdalene thought she was talking with the gardener. Peter and John inspected the blood-stained burial linens, but equated the empty tomb with body theft, not bodily resurrection. The disciples who shuffled sadly toward Emmaus repeated the refrain, 'We had hoped Jesus was the one.'

It's easy to fault these disciples. But then we have the facts of the resurrection too. And when we live in fear, hopelessness, and despair, aren't we acting as if Jesus were still dead and buried instead of living and reigning?

The Lives Easter Changed

But for the first disciples, the reality of the first Easter changed everything. When they finally encountered their risen Lord, their fear turned to confidence and their grief to joy.

Women who had gone to the tomb to anoint Christ's dead body returned home praising their living Lord. The two disciples who had trudged to Emmaus raced back to Jerusalem with the news, "Jesus is alive!" Peter, who out of fear had once denied knowing Jesus, would come to proclaim Him boldly in the very city in which Jesus had been crucified—declaring on the first Pentecost: God raised Jesus "from the dead, freeing Him from the agony of death, because it was impossible for death to keep its hold on Him," Acts 2:24.

Consider how Easter changed Mary Magdalene's life. Here was a woman who loved Jesus; who remained steadfastly beneath His cross on Good Friday, when most of His male disciples had forsaken Him.

Yet, when Jesus died on that cross, Mary's hopes were crushed—so crushed that Mary failed to acknowledge the two angels in Christ's tomb, or even recognize the risen Lord suddenly standing behind her. "Woman," Jesus said, "why are you crying? Who is it you are looking for?" And Mary replied, "Sir, if you have carried Him away, tell me where you have put Him, and I will get Him."

Jesus answered, "Mary." One simple word. And in that one instant everything changed for Mary. Her Savior was alive again, and so were her hopes. Frankly, I cannot read this portion of Scripture without being swept up in the joy of this reunion between hopeless Mary and her risen Lord. I know the Lord has said the same to me: "Mark, why are you so hopeless? Why are you living your life as a funeral procession? Did you think I was still dead? Did you forget that I am alive forevermore?"

Easter Still Changes Lives

Easter still changes lives in dramatic ways. The Easter narrative summarizes many of these changes in the oft-repeated phrase: "Do not be afraid." Afraid of what? How about death?

Certainly, no one wants to die. But when the hour of death comes, we have no reason to fear. Why? Because Easter has changed everything. Jesus said at a funeral, "I am the resurrection and the life. He who believes in Me will live, even though he dies; and whoever lives and believes in Me will never die," John 11:25-26. And then to prove the validity and power of His words, Jesus stepped before the tomb of dead-and-buried Lazarus and raised him to life—as He will one day raise every believer to eternal life.

But it isn't just future life that the resurrection of Jesus guarantees us. It is also true life in the here and now—what Simon Peter referred to as "living hope" in his First Epistle; living hope in contrast to all the lifeless and transitory things in which we are often tempted to place our hope: fame, fortune, connections, careers, insurance, 401k programs.

These are all destined to pass away, as is the hope placed in them. But Jesus Christ lives forever; the same Jesus Christ who said, "I have come that they may have life, and have it to the full," John 10:10.

Yes, we have the facts of Easter, but too often we miss the meaning of Easter. So allow me to place the meaning into its everyday application: "I used to fear death; but Easter changed everything. I used to grieve hopelessly for lost loved ones; but Easter changed everything. I used to think my marriage was too lost to save; but Easter changed everything. I used to feel utterly alone; but Easter changed everything. I used to worry that my sins might not be forgiven; but Easter changed everything. I used to wonder if God keeps all His promises; but Easter changed everything."

This is what it means to apply the reality and power of Christ's resurrection to our lives. And this is why the apostle Paul wrote in Philippians 3:10, "I want to know Christ and the power of His resurrection."

ENTERING ANOTHER'S STORY

Luke 10:25-37

A story is most meaningful when we enter it; that is, when we identify with the setting, dialogue, plot, and especially the predicament of the characters.

Human lives are stories too. Don't we often say, "So, what's your story?" But when the story is another human life (fact instead of fiction), are we willing to enter it? Are we willing to stop and help with the means we have? These are the questions raised by a story Jesus once told: the *Parable of the Good Samaritan*.

And Who is My Neighbor?

To understand the *Parable of the Good Samaritan* we must also understand why Jesus told it. Luke explains that a legal expert came to Jesus with an important question: "Good Master, what must I do to inherit eternal life?" Not surprisingly, this lawyer's approach to salvation was a legal one. "What must I do?" he asked. "Be nice? Keep the Ten Commandments? Watch my language?"

The legal approach to salvation is also the approach of all manmade religions, from ancient polytheism to modern humanism. Only the Bible teaches that a person is not saved by *doing* but by *believing* in Jesus Christ. The apostle Paul wrote: "For it is by grace you have been saved, through faith—and this not from yourselves, it is the gift of God—not by works, so that no one can boast," Ephesians 2:8-9.

How did Jesus answer the lawyer? By directing him to the very law of God the lawyer professed to keep. And here the lawyer's self-defense began to unravel. If saving himself meant keeping God's law perfectly, and if God's law said, "Love your neighbor as yourself," then there had to be exceptions to the rule. Surely God did not expect him to love people like the hated tax collectors or despised Samaritans. So, seeking to justify himself, the lawyer asked, "And who is my neighbor?" In response, Jesus told the *Parable of the Good Samaritan*.

God Doesn't Do Coincidences

Most of us are familiar with this parable of Jesus, so we are already thinking about the despicable actions of the priest and Levite who "passed by on the other side" without helping the victim. We're shaking our heads and vowing, "Well, if that had been me, I would have stopped to help." But let's not pass too hastily over the words in verse 31: "A priest *happened* to be…"

We may view encounters with people as "by chance." But is there really room for chance or coincidence within the providence of almighty God? Remember that passenger who sat next to you on the airplane? Remember that gaunt, unkempt man on the park bench; dressed in rags, shoulders slumped, head in hands? Remember that distraught coworker; the stranger who visited church; and the deathly pale patient lying in a hospital bed? Were these encounters "by chance," or were they God-given opportunities to enter the story of another human being?

Of course, Jesus could have just as easily made the priest and Levite in the parable a farmer and shepherd; a well-digger and tax collector; a merchant and soldier. Instead, He purposely made these two characters *religious* leaders. Need more be said?

Interestingly, when Jesus told the lawyer in verse 28, "You have answered correctly," the Greek word used was ORTHOS, from which we derive our English word orthodoxy. Having the right confession is essential. But of what worth is the right confession without the right actions and right involvement?

It's always easier to pass by on the other side than to stop and get involved. It's always easier to extend handshakes and say "please sign the guest register" than to visit people at home. It's always easier to pretend we don't notice when Christians stop coming to church, or to ignore the warning signs of a troubled marriage. Not my business. Not my responsibility. Someone else will be coming along to help soon enough. What if Jesus Christ had acted this way?

The Good Samaritan

In this parable it is the despised Samaritan who proves to be the Scriptural example of "love your neighbor as yourself." When he sees the victim lying in the road, he does not ask, "Are you friend or foe; Jew or Samaritan?" He does not pass by on the other side under the pretext of "places to go" and "people to see." Instead, he stops. He risks. He gets personally involved. He invests using his own clothes as bandages; his own wine and oil as disinfectant and balm; his own donkey to transport the victim; and his own money to pay for the victim's recovery at a roadside inn. In other words, the Samaritan entered the story of a complete stranger.

The road from Jerusalem to Jericho stretched seventeen miles through the desolate Judean wilderness. But those seventeen miles can also represent seventeen horrible blocks of an inner city neighborhood; seventeen floors of a rundown apartment building; seventeen forgotten rooms in a nursing home; or the seventeen years a devoted husband or wife cared for a spouse with Alzheimer's.

What makes us willing to walk those seventeen miles, whatever they are? What fills us with such compassion that we are willing to enter the story of another human being? Surely it is the knowledge of the compassionate way in which Jesus Christ entered our lives—and saved us.

FORGIVEN AND FORGIVING

Ephesians 4:29-32

Because God forgives us, we should—what? The answer is obvious, isn't it? The answer flows from the cross of Jesus. Because God forgives us, we should forgive one another. In fact, in Scripture, these two principles are inextricably linked. Jesus taught this connection in the Lord's Prayer, saying, "Forgive us our trespasses, as we forgive those who trespass against us." And the connection is very obvious in Ephesians 4: "Be kind and compassionate to one another, forgiving each other, just as in Christ God forgave you."

But does this mean forgiving another person is easy? No. The size, type, and consequences of an injury; the way we feel about the injurer; and certainly our sinful human nature—all stand in the way of forgiving. Yet, nowhere in the Bible does God say, "Forgive if you are in the mood;" or "Forgive if you can muster the strength;" or "Forgive if you think the person is worth it." God simply says, "Forgive."

Sometimes His directive comes in the form of a gentle, loving encouragement, as in the words of Ephesians 4:29-32. At other times, it comes in the form of a stern warning. Consider Matthew 18 and the *Parable of the Unmerciful Servant*, who refused to forgive as he had been forgiven: " 'You wicked servant,' said the master. 'I canceled all that debt of yours because you begged me to. Shouldn't you have had mercy on your fellow servant just as I had mercy on you?' In anger his master turned him over to the jailers to be tortured, until he should pay back all he owed."

Imagine how Simon Peter, who had asked the question that prompted this parable—"How many times should I forgive my brother when he sins against me?"—must have gulped when Jesus concluded His parable by saying: "This is how My heavenly Father will treat each of you unless you forgive your brother from your heart."

Forgiveness From the Heart

Forgiving from the heart (genuine forgiveness) has three elements: the strength to forgive; the willingness to forgive; and the knowledge of what true forgiveness is. And thankfully, all three of these elements are found in the way God forgives us in Jesus Christ.

It is a sinful world. And where sin exists, there exists the certainty of injuries committed and injuries sustained. Accidentally or deliberately, we all hurt other people, and we are all hurt by other people. And some of these hurts are beyond our personal power to forgive. But they are not beyond God's power. And God never asks us to do anything without empowering us to do it.

Notice something important about Paul's letter to the Ephesians. Before uttering one word about Christian behavior—how we live, speak, grow in knowledge of our salvation; treat our spouse; raise our children; resist temptation; and forgive others—the apostle Paul first devotes three entire chapters to the blessings we have in

Jesus Christ. Over and over the emphasis, connection, and prepositions are the same: *in* Christ, *with* Christ, *through* Christ, *to* Christ, *for* Christ, *from* Christ. Why? Because the strength to forgive does not come from within us. The strength to forgive comes from our connection to Jesus Christ.

Who knows more about forgiveness than the one who hung on the cross and cried out, "Father, forgive them, for they know not what they do?" Who has more power to help us forgive than the one of whom Scripture says, "In Him dwells all the fullness of the Godhead bodily," Colossians 2:9?

However, along with the strength to forgive, we must also have the willingness to forgive. The unmerciful servant in Matthew 18 had the ability to forgive; he simply lacked the willingness. And he lacked the willingness because he lacked a personal appreciation of how much he himself had been forgiven.

What about us? How much has each of us been forgiven? And what did it cost God to forgive us? When we can answer these two questions in the light of Scripture, we will find the willingness to forgive another person.

Finally, to genuinely forgive, we must understand the nature of true forgiveness. And this too is seen in the way God forgives us in Christ. So how does God forgive; and how does God's forgiveness differ from human forgiveness?

If I say "I forgive you," but then remind you of your failings for weeks and years; if I say "I forgive you, but only if you don't repeat the same mistake;" if I say "I forgive you, but this is absolutely the last time"—are these expressions of true forgiveness? No. The first is incomplete; the second, conditional; and the third, limited. What if God were to forgive us this way?

Thankfully, God's forgiveness is complete. God's forgiveness is unconditional; that is, not based on our works or merits (we have nothing to contribute) but rather on the blood of Jesus Christ. And God's forgiveness is limitless.

At the cross of Jesus, we learn to forgive in exactly the same way we've been forgiven.

FORGIVENESS

Psalm 32

Thirteen times within three verses of Psalm 32, David used the personal pronouns "I, me, my." Sin and forgiveness were very personal to him; and they should be to us too.

"My Sin"

Sin is a silly subject to a world which calls right wrong and wrong right. "Sin and guilt," we are told, "are the result of parental scolding and religious programming. Get rid of God, and you'll be rid of guilt." Sadly, even some churches have trivialized or eliminated the subject of sin and accountability to God. Attend, and you'll hear happy words like love, hope, peace, and material prosperity, but rarely a word about sin.

In Psalm 32, however, David speaks clearly of sin. In fact, in the first two verses he uses four separate Hebrew words for sin, each with a different meaning. The first word is PESACH, a transgression. Transgression means to cross a line. The second word is CHATA-AH, a sin, literally meaning "to miss the mark." The third word is A-VON, iniquity, with a root meaning of "twisted or bent." The fourth word is REMI-YAH, meaning falsehood or hypocrisy.

As believers, our sincere desire is to please, serve, and obey the Lord. Yet, can anyone of us say that we have never crossed one of God's lines; never missed one of God's marks; never bent one of God's rules; or never distorted one of God's truths? No need to answer. God does. Speaking of human beings as they are by nature, God says in Psalm 14: "The LORD looks down from heaven on the sons of men to see if there are any who understand, any who seek God. All have turned aside, they have together become corrupt; there is no one who does good, not even one."

"Really, God?" we may think. "But I have never stolen a wallet. I have never killed another human being. I have never committed adultery, as King David did with Bathsheba." No, perhaps not. But have we ever thought about doing such things? In God's eyes there is no difference between a sinful thought and sinful deed.

"My Forgiveness"

The Lord has blessed each of us in many ways. He has given us life and health, families and income; food, clothing, shelter, peace, protection, and the freedom to worship. Today, our hearts will beat an average of 100,000 times. Our lungs will draw in an average of 20,000 breaths. And each heartbeat and each breath are gifts of almighty God.

However, for sinners, there is no greater gift than God's gift of forgiveness. This is why David, when writing Psalm 103—"Bless the LORD, O my soul, and forget not all His benefits"—mentioned the benefit of forgiveness before the healing of diseases.

The word "blessed" in Psalm 32, "Blessed is he whose transgression is forgiven," also has the sense of happiness;

and more literally HAPPINESS-ES, because the Hebrew word is always in the plural. The forgiven person is an abundantly blessed and happy person. And if we are not happy, perhaps we don't understand how much we have been forgiven by God.

Just as David uses four Hebrew words for sin in Psalm 32, he also uses three Hebrew words for forgiveness. The first word, NASAH, forgiven, literally means "to pick up and carry away." The second word, CASAH, means "to cover." And the third word, CHASHAV, means "to not hold against."

When we sin, yet turn to the Lord for forgiveness, He lifts our sins up and carries them away. He covers our sins with the blood and righteousness of Christ—not partially, but completely; not temporarily, but eternally. And He does not charge the sins to our account. Whose account does He charge? Christ's. "Therefore, there is no condemnation for those who are in Christ Jesus," Romans 8:1.

FOUND GRATEFUL

Luke 17:11-19

Jesus was traveling toward Jerusalem and the cross. Along the way, He entered a certain village where He encountered ten lepers who called out loudly from a distance: "Jesus, Master, have pity on us!" Despite going to Jerusalem to suffer and die for the sins of the world—a circumstance that would leave us feeling sorry for ourselves rather than sorry for others—Jesus did have compassion on the lepers and healed them. "Go," He said, "show yourselves to the priests." And as they went, they were cleansed.

Ten lepers were healed, but only one returned to thank Jesus. Sadly, the other nine lepers hurried away without a glance back or single "thank you." What was the difference between the one who returned and the nine who left? The answer lies in Luke 17:15-16, "One of them, when he saw he was healed, came back, praising God in a loud voice. He threw himself at Jesus' feet and thanked Him—and he was a Samaritan."

Certainly, the nine lepers saw that they had been healed too. But that is all they saw. They did not look beyond the miracle to the grace and power of the miracle-worker, Jesus Christ. Had the nine looked upon their healing in the same way as the one, all ten would have returned to praise Jesus. All ten would have shouted out "Thank you, God!" in the same loud voice with which they pleaded for Christ's mercy.

If we don't feel grateful, perhaps we are not seeing the blessings all around us. Perhaps we are not viewing the adversities in our lives in the right way. Do we remember that the most important and lasting blessings in our lives have nothing to do with material wealth or banks accounts or the stock market? Our forgiveness, faith, and eternal salvation. The love of our families and friends. Our health. The sun that warms the day. The rain that waters the crops. The air that fills our lungs and oxygenates our blood. Our bodies so wonderfully made. Ears to hear. Eyes to see. Tongues to speak. Arms to hug. These blessings are all around us and always present—blessings that all the money in the world cannot buy; yet blessings which God gives us freely by grace.

Or stop and think about the difficult circumstances in your life. No, they are never pleasant. But we can learn to give thanks even for these when we view them through the gracious, loving Savior, who pitied and healed those ten lepers and pities and heals us. We can learn to say, "Thank you, Lord, for keeping me close to You; for using difficult circumstances to bring me home to You. I had no idea I had wandered so far away." If the lesson is patience, thank You, Lord. If the lesson is persistence in prayer, thank You, Lord. If the lesson is better choices and priorities, thank You, Lord.

Of all the blessings we have to count and count upon today and every other day of our lives, surely the greatest is the eternal love of God that moved Him to give His only-begotten Son, that "whoever believes in Him shall not perish but have everlasting life."

Lord Jesus, thank You for the precious blood that cleansed us from the leprosy of sin. Thank You for the dreadful wounds that brought us healing. Thank You for the love and compassion that led You to the cross and our eternal redemption. How can we stand beneath the cross of Jesus and still say, "I have nothing to be grateful for?"

Gratitude is one of the great, recurring themes of the Bible. By God's grace and Spirit, may it also be the recurring theme of our lives.

THE GIFTS BENEATH GOD'S TREE

Romans 15:4-13

The most important Christmas gifts cannot be bought with VISA or MasterCard, or from a retail outlet or online. They come from God, as James wrote in his epistle: "Every good and perfect gift is from above." In Romans 15, the apostle Paul mentions five such gifts: PATIENCE, COMFORT, HOPE, JOY, and PEACE.

In the Bible, PATIENCE means more than controlling one's temper. The Greek word Paul uses in Romans 15 literally means "to remain under" difficult circumstances and heavy burdens without giving up or giving in. This is the very opposite of what we mean when we say, "I can't take it anymore."

The word translated as COMFORT means "to call to one's side" for the purpose of encouraging. Remember the times when, as a small child, you fell down and skinned your knees or elbows? What did your mother do? She likely called you to her side; swept you into her arms; kissed your cheeks; dried your tears, and in a soothing voice told you that everything would be all right. This is the picture behind the word "comfort" in Romans 15.

It is also the special work of the Holy Spirit. One of the New Testament names for the Holy Spirit is *Paraclete*, which is almost an exact transliteration of the Greek word for comfort Paul uses in Romans 15. The Holy Spirit comforts us by leading us to Jesus and creating faith in our hearts, along with the certainty that we are the redeemed people of God.

HOPE is certain expectation. In the Bible hope is always based in God; not in self, other human beings, or material possessions. Why? Because God alone is faithful. He is the only one who will never disappoint us. How do we know? He sent His Son Jesus to be our Savior.

Jesus came not only to suffer and die for our sins, but as Paul says in Romans 15, to "fulfill the promises made to the fathers." Christmas is proof positive that God takes His word and promises seriously. He will never break a promise He has made to you.

Christmas JOY has nothing to do with smiles, giggles, or happy faces. Biblical joy is something rooted firmly in Jesus. When our joy is based in Jesus, we will always have occasion for the greatest and deepest kind of joy.

Paul wrote to the Philippians: "Rejoice in the Lord always. I will say it again: Rejoice!" When he penned these words, he was in prison—perhaps with chains biting into his wrists and ankles, shivering in the damp cold, and with rats scuttling past his food and feet. Paul knew the "reason for the season." Then, as now, it is Jesus.

And finally PEACE. When the Bible speaks of peace, it means the real and lasting peace that Jesus achieved between the holy God and sinful mankind; and also the way in which this "peace of God" fills our hearts, enabling us to live at peace amid a hectic, chaotic world.

We can't buy any of these gifts at a store. But God gives them to us freely through His word; as Paul writes in Romans 15: "For everything that was written in the past was written to teach us, so that through endurance and the encouragement of the Scriptures we might have hope."

These are the GIFTS BENEATH GOD'S TREE, the tree of the cross. By God's grace and Spirit, may we open them, live them, and rejoice in them not only at Christmas but every day of our lives.

GOD'S FAMILY PLAN

Galatians 4:4-7

Most of us associate Christmas time with "family time;" a time when parents watch their children open presents; a time when sons and daughters come home from college; a time when grandparents arrive for a visit. Christmas is also a time when we may miss family members the most, whether they've moved away or have been called away by the Lord in His infinite wisdom.

In Galatians 4:4-7, the apostle Paul speaks of Christmas in family terms too: God the Father, who sent His Son into the world; God the Son, who came to redeem the world; and God the Holy Spirit, who brings us to faith through the gospel and adopts us into the family of God. In other words, GOD'S FAMILY PLAN.

God the Father Sent Jesus at Just the Right Time

The apostle Paul writes first, "When the fullness of time was come, God sent forth His Son." The *fullness of time* is an interesting description. Think of years, decades, and centuries filling up a measuring cup until the FULL line is reached.

But as the years were passing, God the Father was not biding time; He was directing time, actively preparing the world for the arrival of His Son. There are many aspects to this divine preparation, and they are far too numerous and complex for human minds to comprehend. But we can certainly see illustrations of the Father's Christmas preparations.

Consider how the Christmas narrative opens in Luke 2: "And it came to pass in those days that there went out a decree from Caesar August that all the world should be taxed." As a direct result of this taxing or census, Joseph, who was of the lineage of King David, was required to travel to Bethlehem with Mary, where she gave birth to Jesus— exactly as promised in the Old Testament book of Micah.

Was this a coincidence? No. It was rather God the Father moving kings and kingdoms, events and individuals, to ensure the birth of Jesus at the right time and in the right place. God always does things at the right time. This is as true of our lives as it was true of the birth of Jesus.

God the Son Came to Redeem Us, that We Might Receive the "Adoption of Sons"

Paul tells us that Jesus was "made of a woman" and "made under the law." In becoming truly human, Jesus was tempted and tested in every way that we are, yet was without sin. Therefore, none of us can rightly say, "God doesn't get it. God doesn't know what I'm going through." He went through it. He carried our infirmities and sicknesses. He paid for our sins. He knew suffering, loss, and betrayal to an extent we will never know them.

By becoming human Jesus willingly placed Himself under the law to live the righteous life we could not live and suffer the eternal punishment we should have suffered. And as Galatians 4:5 states, Jesus did all this for us so that "we might receive the adoption of sons."

I am particularly fond of this Bible concept—adoption, because I was adopted as an infant. I mentioned my adoption years ago in a Sunday sermon. After the service, a parishioner told me, "Pastor, that was a nice sermon. But do you think you should have said that you were adopted?"

I understood what she meant. For years, adoption was treated in a hush-hush manner, not only for the sake of the adopted child but because adoption implied something went wrong: perhaps an unplanned birth or an unwanted child. But as I explained to my parishioner, I've never considered adoption as a cause for shame, but rather as a cause for the greatest joy.

Adoption meant I was wanted. Adoption meant I was chosen. Through adoption I received a real family name, home, and inheritance. Did I deserve this? Did I earn this? No. But my unworthiness and inadequacies only made my adoption all the sweeter.

God has adopted us into His family. We didn't deserve or earn this either. Wouldn't you agree that such grace makes our adoption in Christ all the sweeter?

God the Holy Spirit Adopts Us into the Family of God
It is the Holy Spirit who adopts us into the family of God by means of the gospel. He brings us to faith. He leads

us to believe in Jesus as our Savior. He teaches us to call God "*Abba*, Father."

Abba is an Aramaic word which means exactly what it sounds like in English: "Da-da. Daddy. Dad." This is the expression of the trusting toddler, who knows his heavenly Father will protect him, provide for him, and love him forever.

This then is GOD'S FAMILY PLAN. By grace you are part of God's family. By grace you are part of God's plan.

GONE FISHING

John 21:1-14

After His resurrection, Jesus appeared to His disciples over a period of forty days, showing Himself to be alive by many "infallible proofs," Acts 1:3. None of these appearances were unplanned or coincidental. Jesus chose the times and settings. And each appearance taught the disciples another lesson about the meaning of Christ's resurrection. In John 21 Jesus appeared to His disciples after they'd spent the night fishing, without catching a single fish. What did He teach them?

The Risen Jesus is Always with Us

We're not told why the disciples went fishing that day. Perhaps they were bored or simply wanted to stay busy while waiting for the Lord's next appearance. Regardless, off they went, probably never expecting the risen Lord to appear to them as they fished.

As Christians, we believe that Jesus rose triumphantly from the grave, and take great comfort in His resurrection whether facing our own death or dealing with the death of a loved one.

Yet, do we also see the risen Jesus as personally and powerfully present when we go to work or school; visit the library or buy groceries? He is. The disciples learned this lesson while fishing on Lake Galilee. You and I must learn this lesson too. The risen Jesus is always with us, wherever we go, whatever we do.

The Risen Jesus is the Only Means to True Success

Some of the disciples were professional fishermen. They knew Lake Galilee. They knew boats. They knew the local weather patterns, and the best times and places to fish. Yet, when Jesus asked them if they had caught any fish, they answered "No." The point is, you can have all the experience, intelligence, strength, skill, and charisma in the world and still catch nothing.

Are you fishing for something—peace, contentment, happiness, the certainty of salvation? Have you "caught" anything worth keeping? If the answer is no, could it be that you've gone fishing without Jesus?

If God allows us to go for a long night without catching anything in order to teach us how fruitless Christ-less fishing expeditions are, then praise His holy name. The only means to true success is that which the apostle Paul described in Philippians 4:13, "I can do all things through Christ who strengthens me."

The Risen Jesus Provides Answers in His Word

When the disciples chose their own fishing locations, they caught nothing. But when they heard and obeyed Christ's words—"Cast the net on the right side of the boat, and you will find some"—their net bulged at the seams with fish.

No one needs a theological degree to understand this lesson. The answers to our problems lie in God's word. Yes, nothing can appear more small and outmatched than the family Bible. When we are overwhelmed with serious problems, such advice as "turn to the Scriptures" may sound silly—as silly as "cast the net on the right side," when the disciples had likely cast the net a hundred other places too.

Yet, the word of Jesus proved to be the answer the disciples needed. God's word has the answers we need too. It is really that simple and really that comforting.

Wherever the word of God directs us is always the *right* side of the boat.

GOOD NEWS

Romans 1:1-7

News programs today are filled with bad news: wars, terrorism, crime, unemployment, foreclosures, and natural disasters. Bad news happens in our own lives too. It may be bad news from a doctor about a medical test; or bad news from a financial advisor about a stock portfolio; or bad news from an employer about a job. And when we ask why the world is such a bad news place, the Bible answers with one word: Sin.

Many scoff at the notion of sin, but the apostle Paul makes no apologies when he writes to the Romans: "Therefore, just as sin entered the world through one man, and death through sin, and in this way death came to all men, because all sinned."

In the same letter Paul reminds us that ours is not the ever-evolving world imagined by humanists and evolutionists; rather, it is a frustrating world "in bondage to decay." Decay is the ideal setting for bad news.

Is it any wonder then that the Bible calls the message about Jesus Christ good news? This is what the word "gospel" means. Gospel comes from the Greek word EU-ANG-GELION, which is the basis of our English word EVANGELISM and literally means GOOD NEWS. In

Romans 1:1-7, Paul tells us why the gospel of Jesus Christ is such good news

Good News – The Gospel is from God

In Romans 1:1 Paul writes: "Paul, a servant of Jesus Christ, called to be an apostle and set apart for the gospel of God." Just as Paul was not acting or ministering on his own—he was a servant of Christ; a called apostle—so he was not speaking on his own. Wherever he went, to whomever he spoke, he never preached a 'gospel about Paul.' He did not proclaim a made-up gospel or a gospel based on human philosophies. He tells us clearly that his gospel originated with God.

Why is this good news? Because God is always truthful and utterly reliable; and so is the good news about our Savior, Jesus Christ. Have you ever asked: "How do I know that God loves me? How do I know that my sins are really forgiven? How do I know that I'm saved by believing in Jesus as my Savior?"

You know because the gospel tells you so. And the gospel is from the faithful, infallible, eternally reliable God. This is also why Paul writes in Romans 1:16, "I am not ashamed of the gospel, because it is the power of God for the salvation of everyone who believes." Isn't this good news for a bad news world?

Goods News – The Gospel is All About Jesus

The apostle Paul wrote to young Pastor Timothy: "Christ Jesus came into the world to save sinners—of whom I am the worst." We can hear the humble, personal gratitude in his words. Perhaps it is no surprise then that Paul used the word gospel more than any other New Testament writer. As the apostle clearly states in Romans 1:3, Jesus Christ is the whole substance of the gospel. For the gospel from God is the gospel "regarding His Son."

Why is this good news? Because we can't save ourselves. God's law demands perfection in thought, word, and deed. Often, it's difficult for us to make it through the Lord's Prayer without our minds wandering to the latest worry or next NFL game.

This is why Paul tells us in Romans 3:23-24. "For all have sinned and fall short of the glory of God, and are justified freely by His grace through the redemption that came by Christ Jesus." We are not saved by our doing, but by faith in the doing, dying, and rising of Christ. Isn't this good news for a bad news world?

Good News – Jesus is True Man and True God, and as Such, Our Perfect Savior

In Romans 1:4 Paul gives a concise summary of the gospel message. He says of Jesus: "who as to His human nature was a descendant of David, and who through the Spirit of holiness was declared with power to be the Son of God by His resurrection from the dead."

In His incarnation, Jesus became truly human. As our substitute, He lived the righteous life we could not live and suffered the eternal condemnation we should have suffered. In His resurrection, He not only defeated death for us but declared Himself to be who He had always claimed to be: the Son of God and Savior of Mankind. Can you think of any better news for a bad news world? No.

And it is the salvation won for us by Jesus Christ that makes the greeting with which Paul ends our text the most precious of all greetings: "Grace and peace to you from God our Father and from the Lord Jesus Christ."

HAPPINESS

Psalm 1

When facing problems, we often conclude that God is not interested in our happiness—worse, that God is preventing our happiness. After all, if God cared about our happiness, He would give us THIS and prevent THAT. Yet, do we stop to consider that God may not give us THIS or prevent THAT precisely because He *does* want us to be happy?

The psalmist wrote, "Delight yourself in the LORD, and He shall give you the desires of your heart," Psalm 37:4. Does this sound as if God wants you to be miserable? No. He wants you to be happy. In a real sense He wrote this message in the blood of His own Son, Jesus Christ, and nailed it to the cross. And the type of happiness God wants for you is not the cheap, bargain-based happiness peddled by the world, but all the happiness, wholeness, and fullness found in the biblical word "blessed."

God's Promise of Happiness is for Everyone
"I guess I was never meant to be happy." Have you ever said this? You're not alone. But such a bleak outlook on life is irreconcilable with the happy wisdom of Psalm 1. The first verse of this psalm does not say "happy is the rich man" or "happy is the Harvard man" or "happy is the well-dressed man," but rather "happy is the man"—that is,

happy is EVERYONE who turns to God and follows His Happiness Plan.

Only God's Way Leads to Happiness

Psalm 1 describes two very different approaches to happiness: that of the godly man, verses 1-3; that of the ungodly man, verses 4-5; and in verse 6 the inevitable outcome of each way: "For the LORD knows the way of the righteous, but the way of the ungodly shall perish."

Only God's way leads to happiness. Every other way, no matter how attractive, seemingly harmless, or well-paved, will never result in happiness. If you're on the right path, God's path, be patient. Happiness will come. It cannot be otherwise. Psalm 1 does not state 'The man might possibly be happy,' but 'Happy is the man.'

At Times Happiness Means Saying "No"

The world lives by the mantra, "Whatever makes you happy, man." But Psalm 1 reminds us that saying "no" to some things is as essential to our happiness as saying "yes" to others. "Happy is the man who walks not in the counsel of the ungodly, nor stands in the path of sinners, nor sits in the seat of the scornful," Psalm 1:1.

Listening to bad advice, visiting bad places, and keeping bad company will never bring happiness but harm. To think otherwise is to jeopardize our happiness and endanger our faith. "Oh, c'mon. It's only one little step down the Ungodly Path." Yes, but as Psalm 1 makes clear, a step can lead to walking, walking to standing, standing to sitting, sitting to staying, and staying to perishing.

Happiness Comes from a Deep, Daily Study of Scripture

Of the happy man Psalm 1 states, "He delights in the law of the LORD, and in His law he meditates day and night," Psalm 1:2. "Law" in this verse refers to all of God's word, not simply the commandments. And the Hebrew word translated "meditates" literally means "to study while mumbling"—that is, talking to oneself while deeply contemplating the meaning of Scripture.

The deeper we dig into Scripture, the more treasures we unearth. The more treasures we unearth, the more blessed we are. The more blessed we are, the happier we will be.

HEALING IN HIS WOUNDS

Luke 24:36-49

My father, Paul Weis, was in the army infantry in World War II. During the infamous Battle of the Bulge, he was wounded by artillery shrapnel and spent three weeks in an army hospital before rejoining his unit. The injury left a scar on his left leg. As a boy, I often pestered, "Dad, can I see the scar?" Somehow, that scar seemed to summarize the entire war. Every scar tells a story.

The wounds in Christ's hands and feet tell a story too; the story of love, mercy, and compassion so great that Jesus willingly suffered crucifixion in order to redeem us. As the prophet Isaiah said, in His wounds we find healing.

It was Easter evening. Instead of celebrating, the Lord's disciples were hiding behind locked doors. They thought Jesus was dead. If true, they had every reason to fear. They could still recall the mob's "Crucify Him!" They were now enemies of both Church and State.

If Jesus could be crucified, why not His disciples? Had He not told them, "If they persecuted Me, they will persecute you also?" Yet, suddenly, into that setting of tears, fears, and doubts, Jesus came. His first words to His frightened disciples were "Peace be with you." And to give them peace, He showed them His hands and feet. He showed them His wounds.

Hiding behind locked doors seems a perfect metaphor for the way too many of us lead our lives. Our tears, fears, and failures lock us in, transforming us into emotional recluses, if not literal ones. But is this the way Jesus wants us to live? No. This is why Jesus went into that locked room. This is why Paul wrote to the Galatians, "It is for freedom that Christ has set us free."

You may be locked in by a past injury, unable to forgive and move on. Did you know that one of the New Testament words for forgiveness means "to let go?" Unfortunately, if we cannot let go of a past injury, it won't let go of us.

But into such a locked room Jesus comes, speaks His words of peace, and then shows us the wounds in His hands and feet. In His wounds we learn how much God has forgiven each of us and find the strength and will to forgive others. 'Forgive each other, just as in Christ God forgave you,' Paul wrote to the Ephesians.

You may be locked in by present circumstances—a difficult situation, difficult job, or difficult marriage. You may feel as if you cannot go on. Yet, into such a locked room Jesus comes, speaks His words of peace, and shows us His wounds.

What story do His wounds tell? The story of the one love that refused to weary or give up. In those very wounds we find healing and the strength to press on. The writer to the Hebrews encouraged, "Let us fix our eyes on Jesus, the author and perfecter of our faith, who for the joy set before

Him endured the cross, scorning its shame, and sat down at the right hand of the throne of God. Consider Him who endured such opposition from sinful men, so that you will not grow weary and lose heart."

You may be locked in by the future; or more properly said, you may find the future locked to you, as it is to all of us. As mortals, we cannot peer one fraction of a second into the future much less a minute, hour, or day. So often we say, "Nothing will work out for me. I will never find happiness."

But the wounds of Jesus tell a different story, don't they? It is the grace, love, and favor of God so clearly visible in the wounds of Jesus that enable us to say with the apostle Paul—not "I doubt if things will ever work out," but rather, "We know that in all things God works for the good of those who love Him."

You may be thinking, "Yes, this is all well and good. But my life would be so much easier if I could just see Jesus; if Jesus would appear in my living room, as He appeared in the locked room of the disciples; if I could only touch the wounds in His hands, feet, and side.

Yet, it was this very type of thinking that Jesus rebuked when He told the Emmaus disciples, "How foolish you are, and how slow to believe all that the prophets have spoken."

Yes, Jesus showed His disciples His hands and feet. But even more so, He directed them to His healing word.

HIGHER EDUCATION

1 Corinthians 2:6-13

When we hear the word wisdom, we often think of I.Q. quotients, rocket scientists, or the "wise men, scholars, and philosophers" Paul mentions in 1 Corinthians 1:20. Corinth was relatively close to Athens; and Athens was home to many of the ancient world's most renowned philosophers: Socrates, Plato, and Aristotle.

While earthly ideas and philosophies may be a form of wisdom, they are not what God calls wisdom. According to Scripture, the highest form of education comes from the Most High God, who says in Isaiah 55: "For My thoughts are not your thoughts, neither are My ways your ways. As the heavens are higher than the earth, so are My ways higher than your ways and My thoughts than your thoughts." So how does God's wisdom differ from human wisdom?

God's Wisdom is Absolute and Unchanging
Few Bible passages are more comforting than these: Malachi 3:6, "I the LORD do not change;" Hebrews 13:8, "Jesus Christ is the same yesterday and today and forever;" and James 1:17, "Every good and perfect gift is from above, coming down from the Father of the heavenly lights, who does not change like shifting shadows."

Why are these passages so comforting? They tell us God does not change. He is never for us one day and

83

against us the next. He is never unfaithful, never in a bad or unpredictable mood, and never goes back on His word. There is never a doubt about the way God feels about sin or how sinners are saved. "For the wages of sin is death, but the gift of God is eternal life in Jesus Christ our Lord," Romans 6:23.

But is human wisdom absolute or unchanging? If you were to type the word "wisdom" into an internet search engine like Google—I know because I did—the result would be millions of different websites with different ideas about wisdom. Which is correct? Which are you willing to believe? To which are you willing to entrust your salvation, happiness, and the eternal well-being of your children?

Human Wisdom Views God's Wisdom as Foolishness
In 1 Corinthians 1:18 Paul writes, "For the message of the cross is foolishness to those who are perishing." Why foolishness? A poor, humble, and crucified Savior does not fit the human concept of a conqueror or conquering. A God who came to serve; who exercised His almighty power to help others instead of Himself; and who willingly died for His enemies; makes no sense to human wisdom. Nor does the foolishness of preaching.

And honestly, at times, doesn't the notion of preaching the gospel seem a little weak and a little foolish to us? After all, consider the problems we may face: job loss, illness, divorce, accidents, betrayal, rejection, loss of a loved one. Yet, Sunday after Sunday we bring our problems to church and listen to the pastor preach. And the biblical message never changes: God loves you. God has redeemed you through the sacrifice of His Son, Jesus Christ. God is faithful and will bring you safely to His heavenly kingdom.

"Well, that's just talk," the world says. "Just words." Think so? God doesn't; as we are told in 1 Corinthians 1:21, "For since in the wisdom of God the world through its wisdom did not know Him, God was pleased through the foolishness of what was preached to save those who believe."

Preaching Christ crucified might appear to be a small, insignificant thing; but through this small, insignificant thing God exercises all power in heaven and on earth to bring lost sinners to repentance and faith in Jesus Christ. And the fact that God accomplishes this miracle through that which human wisdom considers foolishness is only a further testament to His glory and power.

God's Wisdom is Only Revealed Through the Holy Spirit

I enjoy watching the Discovery Channel. The photography is often spectacular, the subject matter intriguing. I particularly like documentaries on the wonders of the world—the rich and varied forms of life; the miracle of birth; the complexity of the human body; the vastness and grandeur of the universe.

As I watch these programs, I can't help but recall the words of Psalm 104:24, "How many are Your works, O LORD! In wisdom You have made them all." And then inevitably, as the documentary ends, an announcer insists that the universe and everything in it were formed by blind, random chance through the process of evolution. It's all I can do not to hurl something at the TV. Even then I usually stand and shout, "What's wrong with you? How can you say that? You just watched the same program I watched. How can you arrive at such a different conclusion?"

The answer is found in 1 Corinthians 2:10, "No eye has seen, no ear has heard, no mind has conceived what God has prepared for those who love Him, but God has revealed it to us by His Spirit"—something for which we should drop to our knees and thank God with every breath. For without the Holy Spirit, we ourselves would never acknowledge God as our Creator or Jesus Christ as our Savior. "No one can say, 'Jesus is Lord,' except by the Holy Spirit," 1 Corinthians 12:3.

HOW OFTEN SHALL I FORGIVE?

Matthew 18:21-35

"Lord, how often shall my brother sin against me and I forgive him?" This question of Simon Peter is not surprising given the immediate context of Matthew 18. Jesus had just introduced the subject of church discipline, using the words, "If your brother sins against you."

While church discipline may not be an easy or pleasant subject, its purpose, as outlined by Jesus, is to lead an impenitent Christian to repentance and forgiveness. "If he listens to you," said Jesus, "you have won your brother over."

Peter's follow-up question was one of practicality—to paraphrase: 'If my brother comes to his senses and asks me for forgiveness, how often should I forgive him?" Of course, implied in this question is the all-too-human notion that forgiveness must have a limit.

"How often shall I forgive?" This is an important question, and not only within the context of church discipline but also our daily lives. As Paul wrote to the Romans, "For none of us lives to himself, and no one dies to himself," Romans 14:7. And while these words apply most directly to our relationship with the Lord, they also apply to our relationships with each other. We interact with others. And in this sinful world, such interactions provide ample opportunities for hurting others and being hurt by others. So, how often should we forgive?

For Christians, the answer to this question should be obvious. Forgiveness is the reason Jesus suffered, died, and rose again, as Paul wrote to the Ephesians: "In Him we have redemption through His blood, the forgiveness of sins," Ephesians 1:7.

Forgiveness is the reason we may approach God with freedom and confidence. Forgiveness is what God offers us through the Means of Grace—in the gospel, in baptism, and in the Lord's Supper. The authority to forgive and retain sins is an authority bestowed by Christ Himself. In short, everything we are, possess, and anticipate as Christians is due solely to God's forgiveness in Jesus Christ. As Martin Luther said, "Where there is forgiveness of sins, there is also life and salvation."

How can people who are forgiven so much choose to forgive so little? This is the point of the parable Jesus told about the unmerciful servant. The same servant whose king forgave a massive debt of ten million dollars refused to forgive a fellow servant's modest debt of a few dollars. When the king heard of this, he called the servant and said to him, "You wicked servant. I forgave you all that debt because you begged me. Should you not also have had compassion on your fellow servant, just as I had pity on you?"

The unmerciful servant was then delivered to torturers "until he should pay all that was due him." Jesus concluded this parable by saying, "So My heavenly Father also will do to you if each of you, from his heart, does not forgive his brother his trespasses."

Of course, God is the King in this parable; the God who daily and richly forgives us our sins—completely, unconditionally, freely, gladly; knowing full well we have not so much as a cent or "denarii" with which to repay Him.

Refusing to forgive others means that we don't understand or appreciate how much God has forgiven us. So, how often shall we forgive? Simply put, as often as we are asked. For this is how God forgives us.

HOW THE KINGDOM OF GOD GROWS

Mark 4:26-34

The kingdom of God has nothing to do with earthly kings, visible kingdoms, or geographic locations with specific boundary lines. Jesus taught, "The kingdom of God does not come with your careful observation, nor will people say, 'Here it is,' or 'There it is,' because the kingdom of God is within you." Simply put, the kingdom of God is God's gracious rule within the human heart. How does this kingdom grow?

We Scatter the Seeds

Mark 4 opens with the *Parable of the Sower and the Seed.* When the Lord's disciples failed to understand its meaning, Jesus explained that the seed in this parable stood for the word of God. "The farmer sows the word," He said in Mark 4:13. So in all three parables of Mark 4—the *Sower and Seed,* the *Growing Seed,* and the *Mustard Seed*—the seed represents the word of God.

As Christians, you and I have but one role in the growth of God's kingdom. That role is not to form Political Action Committees or Standing Armies, but to "scatter the seed" of God's word.

Each time you comfort a mourner with the Scriptures, or read a family devotion, or remind your children how much

God loves them and what God has done to redeem them in Jesus Christ, you are scattering the seed of God's word. If you don't view the scattering of this seed as a privilege and serious responsibility, consider how faith is created and nourished: "Faith comes through hearing, and hearing by the word of God," Romans 10:17.

God Makes the Seeds Grow

In the *Parable of the Growing Seed*, what part did the farmer play in making the seed grow? None. Notice what Jesus said: "A man scatters seed on the ground. Night and day, whether he sleeps or gets up, the seed sprouts and grows, though he does not know how. All by itself"—the Greek word is AUTOMATOS, the source of our English *automatic*—"the soil produces the grain," Mark 4:26-28.

A seed does not grow because of us but in spite of us. The same is true of the seed of God's word. Just as the power to grow lies in the seed itself and not in the farmer, so also the power to grow faith, heal, and change behavior lies not in the person who shares the word of God, but rather in the word of God being shared.

Using language strikingly reminiscent of Mark 4, the apostle Paul wrote to the Corinthians: "I planted the seed, Apollos watered it, but God made it grow. So neither he who plants nor he who waters is anything, but only God, who makes everything grow," 1 Corinthians 3:6-7.

At times, the word of God can appear so small when compared to life's biggest headaches, heartbreaks, and problems. Isn't this implied in the *Parable of the Mustard Seed*? What appears smaller, more ordinary, and less promising than a mustard seed? The same can be asked of the family Bible. Yet, there is no greater power on earth to make things grow, whether a struggling faith or a struggling marriage or a struggling congregation. As Paul wrote in Romans 1:16, "I am not ashamed of the gospel, because it is the power of God for the salvation of everyone who believes."

How does the kingdom of God grow? We scatter the seeds. God makes the seeds grow. The reality is, you believe in Jesus as your Lord and Savior because sometime, somewhere, someplace, someone planted a gospel seed in you.

And God made it grow.

IN THE "I" OF THE STORM

Matthew 14:22-33

I was a small boy when Hurricane Donna struck Florida in 1960. I can still remember the howling wind, rattling doors and windows, snapping trees, and torrential downpours. But what impressed me most about that storm was its "eye"—a cone of quiet, calm, and safety at the center of the hurricane.

If this is true meteorologically, it is even truer scripturally. Matthew 14:22-33 describes another storm and another place of calm and safety at its center; not an "eye" but the "I" of the storm, Jesus Christ, who said: "Take courage. It is I. Don't be afraid."

Storm Forecast

It had been an exhausting day for the disciples. Crowds flocking to Jesus for miracles. The feeding of the five thousand, at which the disciples had been servers and afterwards had collected leftovers. They must have been grateful when Jesus told them to "get into the boat and go ahead of Him to the other side."

Envision the scene. Late afternoon. Calm lake. Beautiful sunset. Smooth sailing. Then the storm hit and everything went wrong. Fair skies became foul weather. Lazy oaring became desperate rowing. And where was Jesus?

Lake Galilee is known for sudden storms. But so is life. Hurricane Fear. Hurricane Doubt. Hurricane Debt. Hurricane Divorce. Hurricane Death. Some storms begin as a small disturbance; and others with unexpected gale-force opposition. But we've all experienced them. How do we prepare for them?

Storm Preparation

How do we prepare for storms in nature? By having the right supplies available: Canned goods, bottled water, flashlights, candles, portable radio, batteries, first-aid essentials, and so on.

How do we prepare for the storms of life? By building our lives on the rock-solid foundation of God's word. This was the point of Christ's *Parable of the Wise and Foolish Builders* in Matthew 7: "Therefore everyone who hears these words of Mine and puts them into practice is like a wise man who built his house on the rock. The rain came down, the streams rose, and the winds blew and beat against that house; yet, it did not fall, because it had its foundation on the rock." Going to church, attending Bible class or Sunday school, having family devotions—think of all these as storm preparation and foundation-building.

Sometimes the best preparation for a future storm is a past one. Am I suggesting that storms may serve a useful purpose in life? Yes. Should we be storm-chasers? No. Are storms pleasurable experiences? Only if we are inside looking out. Nevertheless, if the same storm that reveals my weaknesses also reveals the limitlessness of God's power and grace, hasn't that storm served a useful purpose?

God teaches us through His word. However, at times, God also teaches us through storms. If you find this difficult to believe, consider Matthew 14:22, "Immediately *Jesus* made the disciples get into the boat and go on ahead of Him to the other side, while He dismissed the crowd." Who made the disciples get into the boat? Jesus. Who told the disciples to cross the lake? Jesus. Who knew the storm was coming? Jesus. Who allowed the disciples to strain at the oars from dusk until dawn? Jesus. Who invited Peter to walk on water, knowing full well that he would sink in doubt? Jesus.

And why would Jesus permit such a storm in nature and storm of spirit? To teach His disciples the importance of trusting solely in Him; of seeing Him as the "I" of every storm. Peter was able to walk on water, to do the impossible, only because of Jesus Christ. Peter was saved from drowning only by Jesus Christ. And where did Peter learn these lessons? Not in school. In a storm.

Storm Aftermath

If you had seen Jesus command wind and waves, would you ever doubt His ability to save you from any storm in life? If you had seen Jesus feed five thousand using five loaves of bread and two small fish, would you ever doubt His ability to put food on your table or clothes on your back? If you had seen Simon Peter walk on water through the power of Christ, would you ever doubt the Savior's ability to help you through impossible situations?

But you have seen these things in the pages of Scripture. So the only remaining questions are: Is Scripture true or not? Did Jesus calm the storm or not? Did Jesus enable Peter to walk on water or not? Did Jesus immediately save Peter from drowning or not?

If you answered "Yes" to even one of these questions— and you should have answered "Yes" to all of them—then you have no reason to doubt that Jesus will save you from your storms as well.

When Jesus is the "I" of each storm, we will find calm, quiet, and safety though the storm rages all around us. The wind and waves will disappear. The boat will immediately reach its destination. And in the aftermath of each storm, we will say of Jesus: "Truly, You are the Son of God!"

JESUS IS COMING!
ARE YOU READY?

Matthew 24:37-44

Advent means *coming*. During the church season of Advent, we focus on the coming of our Lord Jesus Christ: His coming at Christmas to save mankind; His coming at the end of time to judge all humanity; and His coming into the human heart through the power of the Holy Spirit.

In view of these comings, a secondary theme of Advent is the preparation to receive Jesus. What preparations would you make if you were expecting a visit from a world leader or famous celebrity? Clean the house? Polish the silverware? Get a different hairstyle?

The one of High Birth whom we await is none other than the living God. And preparations for His arrival have nothing to do with cleaning the house, but rather cleaning the heart; as the Psalmist writes: "Create in me a clean heart, O God; and renew a right spirit within me."

But how certain are we that Jesus will return? Jesus did say three times in Revelation, "Behold, I am coming soon!" And the writers of the New Testament echoed this sense of urgency. Paul wrote in Romans 13, "The night is nearly over; the day is almost here." Simon Peter wrote in his First Epistle, "The end of all things is near." John wrote in his First Epistle: "Dear children, this is the last hour."

Yet, more than two thousand years have passed. Where is Jesus? Why hasn't He returned? Has He forgotten about us? Did He find something better to do? No. Four times within Matthew 24:37-44, Jesus assures us that He is returning. And the return of Christ is so central to our Christian faith and expectations that twenty-four of the twenty-seven books in the New Testament speak of His second coming.

But when will the Lord return? Despite the Lord's clear warning in Matthew 24 that "no one knows about that day or hour, not even the angels in heaven," to this very day people continue to predict the exact date and time of Christ's return, and often to the great harm of those who listen to them.

Remember the Heaven's Gate cult, whose members believed that God was returning for them on an asteroid, and killed themselves in order to meet Him? Remember all the dire predictions about Y2K, the year 2000 A.D.? Did you know that a similar panic occurred in the year 1000 A.D.? Many believed that the year 2012 would usher in the end of time—this because 2012 coincided with the end of the Mayan Calendar and a rare alignment of planets. Such speculation never ends. And it is never right.

The best answer to the question of when Christ will return is the biblical answer; namely, "at any time." While we may not know the exact date or time, Jesus did give us signs by which to identify the approaching end of the world: The appearance of false Christs and false prophets; wars and rumors of wars; great earthquakes in various places;

pestilences and pandemics; severe famines and economic hardship; and on a more positive note, the worldwide reach of the gospel. Jesus said, "And this gospel of the kingdom will be preached in the whole world as a testimony to all nations, and then the end will come."

All of these end-time signs are as commonplace today as the six o'clock news; and as Jesus prophesied, they are happening with the increasing intensity and frequency of labor pains. From this we may rightly conclude that the end of the world and the return of our Savior are rapidly approaching. This is the reason Jesus said: "So you also must be ready, because the Son of Man will come at an hour when you do not expect Him."

Jesus is coming. Are you ready?

JOYFUL, PRAYERFUL, THANKFUL

1 Thessalonians 5:16-18

In 1 Thessalonians 5:16-18 the Greek verbs "be joyful" and "pray" and "give thanks" are in the present tense and the imperative mode. The present tense was used to describe ongoing action, and the imperative mode was used to convey strong commands. So by themselves these three verbs mean: "Go on rejoicing! Go on praying! Go on giving thanks!"

However, the apostle Paul was still not satisfied. He added the modifiers "always, continually," and "in all circumstances;" and then he placed the modifiers in positions of emphasis within the sentences. In essence, the apostle Paul combined four grammatical techniques— verb tense, verb mode, modifiers and their positions—to emphasize the same message; namely, the Christian life is to be characterized by ongoing joy, prayer, and thanksgiving.

You may be thinking, "But how? How can I always be joyful, prayerful, and thankful? This is a human impossibility." And you are right. It is humanly impossible. Had Paul stopped with these directives, his words would have had no more power than a Hallmark greeting card or locker room pep-talk. But he did not stop with "be joyful always" and "pray continually" and "give thanks in all circumstances." He went on to tell us how, saying, "For this is God's will for you *in Christ Jesus*."

These are important words. When things go wrong in our lives, we too often conclude that God wants us to be miserable or God wants us to suffer. Nothing could be farther from the truth. To the contrary, as Paul wrote, God wants us to be joyful, prayerful, and thankful. And what God wills for us He gives to us freely in His Son, Jesus Christ.

No matter what the question, the apostle Paul saw Jesus Christ as the only answer. How do we live joyful, prayerful, and thankful lives? In Jesus Christ. How do we know that we are saved? In Jesus Christ. How do we sustain a Christian marriage? In Jesus Christ.

How do we carry out a gospel ministry? In Jesus Christ. How do we deal with loss or illness? In Jesus Christ. How do we go on rejoicing, hoping, caring, and triumphing, no matter what our condition in life—sickness or health, poverty or wealth, the vigor of youth or the challenges of age? In Jesus Christ.

Always being joyful, prayerful, and thankful does not mean that we go through life with a manufactured smile on our lips, or that we never hurt or fail or cry. Rather, it means that when we believe in Christ as our Lord and Savior, we always have something—better said, Someone—of eternal worth to rejoice, pray, and be thankful about.

When Paul wrote "Rejoice in the Lord always," he wasn't sitting in an air-conditioned study, surrounded by bookshelves. He was in a filthy, damp, rat-infested prison.

And there, without one Christmas card, one Christmas tree, or one Christmas present, he declared, "I can do everything through Him who gives me strength."

KNOW THYSELF, NO THYSELF

Mark 8:27-38

"KNOW THYSELF" was written on the ancient temple of Apollo in Delphi, Greece, and became a cornerstone of western philosophy. Know yourself. Know who you are. Know your strengths and weaknesses. Today, consider a similar phrase but with a different "know;" not KNOW THYSELF but NO THYSELF. Say "no" to yourself.

This is the "no" Paul wrote about in Titus 2:11-12, "For the grace of God that brings salvation has appeared to all men. It teaches us to say 'No' to ungodliness and worldly passions, and to live self-controlled, upright and godly lives."

This is also the "no" Jesus spoke about in Mark 8:34, saying, "If anyone would come after Me, he must deny himself and take up his cross and follow Me." To deny oneself is to say "no" to oneself. And the connection between these two phrases, KNOW THYSELF and NO THYSELF is simply this: When we KNOW what Jesus Christ willingly sacrificed to save us from our sins, we should willingly say NO to self, selfishness, and a sinful way of life.

Saying "No" is Painful, but Necessary

Self-denial is necessary even in earthly pursuits. No one ever became an Olympic champion by lying on the sofa and watching TV. It takes years of rigorous training and saying "no" to self. If I want to lose weight, I must say "no" to certain unhealthy foods and exercise regularly. If I want a happier, healthier marriage, I must focus less on self and more on spouse. Saying "yes" to one thing means saying "no" to another.

If this is true of earthly goals, why would we think it different for heavenly ones? It isn't different. This is why Jesus said, "If anyone would come after Me, he must deny himself." We cannot say "yes" to Jesus without saying "no" to ourselves. We cannot claim, "Jesus, You are the Lord of my life," while simultaneously claiming, "It's my life, Jesus; I will do what I want." And we cannot follow Jesus without coming into conflict with the world. "If they persecuted Me, they will persecute you also," warned Jesus in John 15:20.

When Jesus spoke openly of His approaching suffering, death, and resurrection—"the Son of Man must suffer many things; must be killed and after three days rise again," Mark 8:31—Peter took Jesus aside and began to rebuke Him. Some churches do the same today. "No, Jesus, we cannot have any unhappy talk about suffering, sacrifice, or self-denial, whether Yours or ours, because Sunday attendance and offerings will decrease."

While Peter's intentions were good, Jesus told him in no uncertain terms that a theology devoid of Christ's suffering, death and resurrection is not from God but from Satan: "Get behind Me, Satan! You do not have in mind the things of God, but the things of men," Mark 8:33.

In God's plan of salvation, it would be through Christ's suffering and death—His saying "no" to Himself and "yes" to us—that the world would be saved. In the same way, we cannot talk about following Jesus without acknowledging that following Him may result in hardship. Why do it then?

Saying "No" Voluntarily is Grounded in Christ's Love and Sacrifice

Our willingness and ability to deny ourselves is grounded in Christ's great love and sacrifice for us. This is very apparent in our text. Before ever mentioning the "cross" you and I may carry for the sake of following Jesus, Jesus first mentioned the cross He would bear for us; the cross that only He could bear. "He then began to teach them that the Son of Man must suffer many things and be rejected by the elders, chief priests and teachers of the law, and that He must be killed and after three days rise again," Mark 8:31.

It is the full and free salvation that we have in Jesus Christ that enables and empowers us to say "no" to ourselves and "yes" to God. As Paul wrote, "The grace of God that brings salvation to all men...teaches us to say 'No.'"

LIFE THROUGH THE HOLY SPIRIT

Ezekiel 37:1-14

The *Valley of Dry Bones* was more than scenery. It was also a graphic picture of Israel's hopelessness. God told Ezekiel, "Son of Man, these bones are the whole house of Israel. They say, 'Our bones are dried up and our hope is gone; we are cut off,'" Ezekiel 37:11.

From a human perspective, the Israelites had good reason for hopelessness. The majority were captives in Babylon. Their beloved Jerusalem was rubble. Their holy temple, the place of God's dwelling among His people, lay in ruins.

And the *Valley of Dry Bones* vividly illustrated this utter hopelessness. Consider what Ezekiel saw: not a small boneyard, but a vast valley filled with bones; not fully preserved skeletons, but broken, scattered bones; not fresh bones—at least some semblance of recent life—but bones baked dry and bleached white by the merciless sun.

Periodically, we too traipse through boneyards of broken hearts, homes, and hopes. And when we do, God asks us the same question He asked Ezekiel: "Son of man, can these bones live?" Can there be hope amid hopeless circumstances? Can the Lord mend what is broken and put our lives back together in just the right way? Of course He can. But it is important for us to know how God does this;

namely, through the Holy Spirit, who gives life, hope, joy, and wholeness through the word of God.

The dry bones of Ezekiel 37 only came to life when Ezekiel spoke the word of God to them; the same word through which the Holy Spirit connected the bones in the right way; covered the bones with tendons, ligaments, and skin; and changed the bones into a living, breathing army ready to do battle in the name of the Lord. And life and hope would come to the people of God in the same way. After telling Ezekiel to "prophesy" to the bones, God told him to "prophesy" to the Israelites.

Who is it that fills us with hope? Who is it that empowers us to go on when we don't have the strength or will to go on? Who is it that puts the broken, disjointed parts of our lives together again and makes us whole? The Holy Spirit working through the word of God. This is the lesson of Ezekiel 37:1-14. This is also the meaning of Pentecost; the outpoured Holy Spirit, who enabled poor, uneducated fishermen to proclaim the "wonders of God" in multiple languages and set their tongues on fire to preach Jesus Christ.

Oh, that the Spirit would set our tongues on fire in the same way. If we want to "breathe life" into our own hopeless nation, the answer is not to form a Political Action Committee, but to share the word of God and let the life-giving Holy Spirit do His work.

If we are struggling with a troubled marriage or troubled conscience, the answer is not to surrender, but to share the word of God and let the life-giving Holy Spirit do His work. If we are worried about the size of our congregation, the answer is not to lose hope, but to share the word of God and let the life-giving Holy Spirit do His work.

Whatever "dem dry bones" are in your life, let them hear the word of the Lord. For this is what the Sovereign Lord says: "I will put my Spirit in you and you will live," Ezekiel 37:14.

LIFETIME

Psalm 139

God Knows Us Completely

God knows everything about us. And His knowledge of us encompasses every detail of our lives, including when we sit and stand, and when we wake and sleep. He even knows what we are going to say before we say it. And God has known all these details about us from eternity. No wonder David exclaimed: "Such knowledge is too wonderful for me, too lofty for me to attain," Psalm 139:6.

That God knows us completely is both sobering and comforting. Sobering, because God knows our every thought, word, and deed. Comforting, because God knows our needs before we present them; and He never confuses our needs with our wants. And God's knowledge of us is not merely intellectual, it is also *experiential*. When Jesus Christ, God the Son, came to be one of us, He also became one with us in our human experiences—without our sin. Consequently, we can never rightly say, "God doesn't know what I'm going through." He does know, because He is omniscient and because He Himself went through it.

God is Always with Us

Remember the story of Joseph? Here was a young man whose circumstances went from bad to worse. He was resented by his own brothers, cast into an empty cistern, and sold into slavery. When he refused to sleep with Potiphar's wife, he was unjustly sentenced to prison. And yet we read of Joseph, "But while Joseph was there in prison, the LORD was with him," Genesis 39:20. Throughout Joseph's lifetime, God was with him. And throughout our lifetime, God is with us too.

When facing problems, we're often tempted to think, "God has forsaken me." But as David wrote in Psalm 139, God is always there for us. "Where can I go from Your Spirit? Where can I flee from Your presence? If I go up to the heavens, You are there; if I make my bed in the depths, You are there. If I rise on the wings of the dawn, if I settle on the far side of the sea, even there Your hand will guide me, Your right hand will hold me fast," Psalm 139:7-10.

God's Power is at Work in our Lives
Psalm 139 alludes to the infinite power of God, especially as revealed in creation, whether the birth of the universe or the birth of a human being. "For You created my inmost being; You knit me together in my mother's womb. I praise You because I am fearfully and wonderfully made," Psalm 139:13-14. I've seen God's power revealed in the vast, starry heavens; in the grandeur of mountains; in the myriad and complex forms of life on Earth. But I've never been more awed by that creative power than when watching the birth of my two sons, Justin and Andrew—so fearfully and wonderfully made.

We may be sick or suffering. We may be struggling to save a marriage. We may be worried about finances or our sins and failings. But God's power is always mightily at work in our lives—the very same power with which He created the universe and raised Jesus Christ from the dead.

God's Love for Us is Eternal

But why would God want to know us? Why would God want to be with us? Why would God want to display His infinite power in our infinitesimally small lives? The answer is, because God loves us. As David wrote in Psalm 139: "How precious to me are Your thoughts, O God! How vast is the sum of them. Were I to count them, they would outnumber the grains of sand. When I awake, I am still with You," Psalm 139:17-18.

There is another way to translate verse 17 of this psalm, namely, "How precious are Your thoughts *about me*, O God." You see, it's not just the way we think about God. It's the precious thoughts He has for us—the undeserved love that moved Him to sacrifice His own Son, Jesus Christ, to redeem us from our sins. This is the divine love that stretches the "little dash" of our lifetime into all the dimensions of eternity.

LIKE FATHER, LIKE CHILDREN

Matthew 5:38-48

Epiphany means "to shine upon." During the church season of Epiphany, it is the glory of Jesus Christ that shines upon us, assuring us that the Baby born in Bethlehem, the Man who died on the cross, was in fact the eternal Son of God and Savior of mankind.

Jesus revealed His glory in different ways; through His miracles and His words. At the conclusion of the *Sermon on the Mount*, those who heard Jesus speak "were amazed at His teaching, because He taught them as one who had authority, and not as their teachers of the law."

But the glory of the Lord is also revealed in another important way; specifically, the way in which we respond to personal injuries and injustices. When we choose to overcome evil with good instead of extracting "an eye for an eye," we glorify God and identify ourselves as His children.

An 'Eye for an Eye' or 'Going the Extra Mile?'

Human nature understands an "eye for an eye." It does not understand "turning the other cheek" or "going the extra mile." From the world's perspective, turning the other cheek means getting slapped twice. Giving the cloak and tunic means getting twice as cold. Going the extra mile means getting twice as tired. We know this because we've experienced it.

Christians are by no means controlled by the old nature. We are led by the Spirit of God. Yet, the old nature remains with us in this life, always urging us on to vengeance; always shouting "Me first" and "I'm all that matters." We recognize its voice. It sounds like this: "Don't let your spouse speak to you that way. She has no right." Or, "You did all the work. Now your coworker is getting all the credit." Or, "Did you see the way that guy cut you off in traffic? And with not so much as a blinker signal or wave of apology. I think we should follow this guy, turn for turn, mile for mile, until we have the chance to cut him off." Sound familiar? Of course it does. But this isn't God talking. It's our sinful human nature.

You Have Heard that It was Said, but I Say to You

Six times within the Sermon on the Mount Jesus corrected the shallow religious interpretations of Israel's religious leaders, including their faulty advice on personal retribution. "Eye for eye" and "tooth for tooth" were part of the Mosaic Law. But this law was given only to Israel's judges and magistrates to ensure that victims received justice and that offenders received fair sentences.

At the time of Jesus, however, the scribes and Pharisees had taken this law and applied it to individuals, encouraging them to pursue private justice. This is what Jesus was objecting to. How did He respond? "Do not resist an evil person. If someone strikes you on the right cheek, turn to him the other also. And if someone wants to sue you and take your coat, let him have your cloak as well. If someone forces you to go one mile, go with him two miles. Give to

113

the one who asks of you, and do not turn away from the one who wants to borrow from you." Striking words, aren't they? But what do they mean?

Be Generous. Give Liberally. Isn't that How Your Heavenly Father Treats You?

When we study these remarkable words of Jesus, it's important not only to understand what He says, but also what He doesn't say. He doesn't say, "Stand perfectly still while someone beats you senseless." He doesn't say, "Give until your pockets and bank account are empty." He doesn't say, "Walk fifty miles or halfway through the Judean wilderness." Each of the examples He gives are *limited* in nature; that is, minor infractions versus major offenses.

Notice what Jesus says about turning the other cheek: "If someone strikes you on the right cheek, turn to him the other also." If I'm facing you; and if I'm right handed (as the majority of people are); and if I strike you on your right cheek, I would have to use the back of my right hand. Interestingly, the Mishna, a collection of Jewish writings available in Christ's day, stated that anyone striking a person with an open palm was subject to a fine. But if a person slapped another with the back of his hand, the fine was to be doubled.

Why? Because a back-handed slap was considered to be a sign of disrespect and contempt. Consequently, these familiar words of Jesus, "turning the other cheek," likely have more to do with a personal insult than a personal injury. Are we willing to tarnish the reputation of our

114

heavenly Father just because our reputation is tarnished? Of course not.

Like Father, Like Children

Jesus is not telling us to ignore evil. He's telling us that, as God's children, we are not to seek personal vengeance. Instead, we are to display a generous, forgiving spirit like that of our Father in heaven.

And in this regard, the supreme example is the Son of God, Jesus Christ—as Simon Peter writes in his First Epistle: "But if you suffer for doing good and you endure it, this is commendable before God. To this you were called, because Christ suffered for you, leaving you an example, that you should follow in His steps. 'He committed no sin, and no deceit was found in His mouth.' When they hurled their insults at Him, He did not retaliate; when He suffered, He made no threats. Instead, He entrusted Himself to Him who judges justly."

LIVING WATER

John 4:1-30

More than two thousand years ago, two strangers met at Jacob's Well in Sychar, Samaria. The time of year was likely summer. According to John 4:6, the time of day was "about the sixth hour," that is, high noon. One of these strangers was a Samaritan woman. We don't know her name, address, or age, only that she had lived a difficult life—five marriages, a sizeable quantity even by modern standards. The other stranger was Jesus Christ, the Son of God.

The conversation that day at Jacob's Well, one of the longest one-on-one conversations of Jesus recorded in Scripture, forever changed this woman's life. The conversation began with Jesus asking the woman for a drink of water. It ended with the woman asking Jesus for "living water," and her recognition of Him as the long-awaited Messiah.

Jesus – Savior of the Lost and Lonely Individual
But was the encounter that day at Jacob's Well merely a coincidence? At first glance, it may seem so—just part of a chance meeting at a "rest stop." Jesus was traveling from Judea to Galilee. Along the way, He grew hot, tired, and thirsty. He happened to be near Jacob's Well. He happened to sit down at the well about noon. A Samaritan woman

happened to come to the well at exactly the same time. Just a coincidence, right?

Wrong. God does not do coincidences. It was no coincidence that Jesus performed His first miracle at a wedding in Cana of Galilee. It was no coincidence that Jesus called Galilean fishermen to be fishers of men. It was no coincidence that Jesus was walking into the village of Nain as a poor, grieving widow was walking out. It was no coincidence that Jesus encountered that Samaritan woman at Jacob's Well.

John 4:1 states that Jesus "had to go through Samaria." Passing through Samaria was the shortest, fastest route from Judea to Galilee; however, it was not the only route. Jesus could have easily crossed the Jordan River to the east, traveled north through Perea, and then crossed the Jordan again into Galilee, avoiding Samaria completely. Consequently, when John 1:4 says that Jesus "had to go through Samaria," the "had to" has nothing to do with coincidence or geography and everything to do with Jesus being our perfect Savior.

Jesus did not cross Samaria to save time. Jesus crossed Samaria to save one lost, lonely woman. Imagine that— the one of whom John writes in chapter one of his gospel, "through Him all things were made"—this same Jesus deliberately walked through Samaria, deliberately sat down at Jacob's well, in order to deliberately save this one individual. When Jesus said in Luke 19:10, "the Son of Man came to seek and to save what was lost," He meant it. It was no coincidence that Jesus sought and saved you either. Isn't this knowledge alone living water for a thirsting soul?

Jesus – Savior of the Whole World

But Jesus had to travel through Samaria for another reason; not only to be the Savior of the individual, but also to be the Savior of the whole world. In going through Samaria, Jesus was traveling to a place few Jews and none of Israel's religious leaders were willing to go. Jews and Samaritans hated each other. Jews believed that Samaritans were beyond even God's power or desire to save.

Jewish rabbis actually taught that it was a sin for a Jew to touch a Samaritan dish. We can hear the surprise in the Samaritan woman's voice when she asks Jesus in John 4:9, "You are a Jew and I am a Samaritan woman. How can You ask me for a drink?"

Think of all the barriers that stood between Jesus and that Samaritan woman. A barrier of gender. In ancient Israel men rarely spoke to women in public. When the Lord's disciples returned that day from buying groceries, they "were surprised to find Him talking with a woman," John 4:27.

Along with gender, there was the barrier of race—the hostility between Jews and Samaritans. There was also a barrier of religious ignorance to which Jesus alludes in John 4:22, "You Samaritans worship what you do not know; we worship what we do know, for salvation is from the Jews."

And finally, the most impenetrable barrier of all, sin. And it is to the knowledge of her sin that Jesus directs the Samaritan woman with His simple request: "Go call your husband and come back," John 4:16. He knew full well that the woman was not married, but simply living with a man.

Yet, it is the love, compassion, and grace of Jesus Christ that breaks through all of these barriers. In first coming to this woman, He draws the woman to Himself. In leading her to the knowledge of her personal sin, He leads her to the knowledge of her personal Savior. In showing this woman her thirst, He satisfies that thirst with the living water of His word.

No matter who we are, where we are from, or what we have done; whether we are male or female, black or white, rich or poor, popular or unknown—the love and salvation of Jesus Christ has embraced and redeemed us all.

How many people do you know right now who are like that Samaritan woman; searching for happiness in all the wrong places; drinking from all the wrong wells—money, possessions, relationships, fame, careers, alcohol, drugs, human promises? Searching, but never finding. Drinking, but never satisfied.

Only the "living water" of Jesus Christ can bring true life. His offer is not merely to quench our thirst, *but to end it*. "Whoever drinks the water I give him will never thirst. Indeed, the water I give him will become in him a spring of water welling up to eternal life," John 4:14.

119

MAJESTY IN MINOR MATTERS

John 2:1-11

All of us go through difficulties. When we do, we're often tempted to doubt God's goodness, wisdom, love, and power. We may ask questions we don't like to ask: Where is God? Why isn't He helping? Does He care? Does He have better, more important things to do?

Yet, the God revealed to us in Scripture loves us beyond measure and is intimately involved in every aspect of our lives, even the "minor matters." This is certainly evident in the wedding at Cana, as recorded in John 2:1-11.

God is Involved
Changing water into wine was a miracle. But the circumstances in which Jesus performed this miracle were no less miraculous. The location of the miracle was not the capital city of Jerusalem or the luxurious palace of Herod, but the sleepy, don't-blink-or-you'll-miss-it town of Cana.

The reason for the miracle was not a national crisis or natural disaster, but a matter as minor as a shortage of wine. Likewise, the recipients of the miracle were not emperors or celebrities, but two newlyweds whose names we don't even know.

What does this teach us—that God is distant and disinterested, or that He is involved in every aspect of our lives, from the largest problems to the smallest headaches? The absolute proof of God's involvement in our lives is in the sacrifice of Jesus Christ for our sins.

God will Act at the Right Time and in the Right Way

Commentators often focus on the mild rebuke Jesus gave Mary: "Woman, what does your concern have to do with Me? My hour has not yet come," John 2:4. Yet, I believe that mild rebuke was also an invitation. By it Jesus was saying, "You've brought this problem—the shortage of wine—to My attention. Now trust Me to act at the right time and in the right way. You know who I am."

Mary understood this, and therefore told the servants: "Whatever He says to you, do it." In other words, Mary expected Jesus to act. Mary expected Jesus to do a miracle. Shouldn't we? He may not act in our hour, but He will always act in *His* hour.

God will Provide an Extraordinary Solution

When you and I are willing to wait for God to act at the right time, in His way, the outcome will always be infinitely greater than anything we could have imagined or accomplished on our own. Abraham had no idea where God was leading him; but at the end of his journey he found himself in the Promised Land. Job went through great heartache and loss. Yet, Scripture describes the end of his life this way: "The LORD blessed the latter part of Job's life more than the first."

Why does this always surprise us? How can we go through our lives thinking "God is out to get me" or "God doesn't care about me," when God has already given us the very best He has to give? And so the apostle Paul wrote: "If God is for us, who can be against us? He who did not spare His own Son, but gave Him up for us all—how will He not also, along with Him, graciously give us all things?" Romans 8:31-32.

Don't leave the wedding of Cana thinking only, "What a beautiful bride," or "What a handsome groom," or "What extraordinary wine." Leave Cana knowing that God will reveal His majesty even in the minor matters of your life.

MINISTERING TO THE LOST

Luke 15:1-32

Luke introduces the parables of the *Lost Sheep, Lost Coin*, and *Lost Son* with the words: "Now the tax collectors and 'sinners' were all gathering around to hear Him. But the Pharisees and the teachers of the law muttered, 'This man welcomes sinners and eats with them,' " Luke 15:1-2.

The scribes and Pharisees were the religious leaders of Israel—the pastors, teachers, youth ministers, and doctors of theology. However, instead of ministering to the lost, they essentially "locked the church doors and turned off the lights." They believed that tax collectors, notorious sinners, Samaritans, and the hated Gentiles were beyond even God's forgiveness. Yet, despite all their learning and religion, they knew little of God's redemptive love for the lost or how lost they were themselves. In the three parables of Luke 15, so richly colored by Christ's own ministry to the lost, we learn four characteristics of true Gospel outreach.

Commitment and Energetic Activity

When the shepherd realized that one sheep was lost, he didn't wait for a more convenient time to search. He went immediately and wholeheartedly. And where did he go? Into the difficult and dangerous terrain of the wilderness.

When the woman realized that one coin was lost, she didn't search halfheartedly or indifferently. She searched carefully and with the same commitment as the shepherd.

And nowhere is this type of personal involvement and energetic activity better exemplified than in the ministry of Christ Himself: "Jesus went through all the towns and villages, teaching in their synagogues, preaching the good news of the kingdom and healing every disease and sickness. When He saw the crowds, He had compassion on them, because they were harassed and helpless, like sheep without a shepherd," Matthew 9:35-36.

Yes, Jesus always welcomed those who came to Him. But His ministry was characterized by 'going,' not 'waiting.' Our Gospel outreach should be the same.

Urgency

Lost-ness comes in many forms and none of them are pleasant. We all know the frustration of losing our way while traveling; or of losing our wallet, car keys, or the TV remote. Serious problems in life—illness, the death of a loved one, job loss, addictions—can leave us feeling far more lost, disoriented, alone, and uncertain of our surroundings. You've heard people say, "I don't know what to do. I feel so lost."

Yet, there is a far worse type of lost-ness. Scripture teaches that all people by nature are lost and condemned; without God and without hope; eternally lost unless they come to know Jesus Christ as their Lord and Savior. This fact alone should lend urgency to our gospel ministries; for the answer to lost-ness is Jesus Christ.

Some of the most familiar and cherished passages of the Bible assure us that in Jesus Christ we will never be lost. John 3:16 states: "For God so loved the world that He gave His one and only Son, that whoever believes in Him shall not perish but have everlasting life." The word "perish" in this verse is the same Greek word for "lost" used in the parables of the *Lost Sheep*, *Lost Coin*, and *Lost Son*.

Rejoicing

Sometimes it is easier to stay with the ninety-nine obedient sheep than to look for the one sheep who wandered away. Sometimes it is easier to minister to people we consider worth the effort rather than to those we consider a waste of time and resources. People in certain neighborhoods. People of certain races or social conditions. People lying in nursing homes or wandering homeless in the streets. "What do they matter? God can't love or want people like that." The scribes and Pharisees said the same of the tax collectors and notorious sinners, but they were wrong.

God does love the lost, the undesirable, the outcasts and misfits; not because they (or we) are worth it, but because of His infinite and amazing grace. The irony is that the accusation the scribes and Pharisees leveled against Jesus—"This man welcomes sinners and eats with them"— was true.

"The Son of Man came to seek and to save what was lost," said Jesus. And as each parable in Luke 15 testifies, God Himself rejoices when even one lost sinner is found; when even one lost sinner repents; when even one lost sinner comes home to God through faith in Jesus Christ.

Personal Gratitude

The apostle Paul shared the gospel of Jesus Christ virtually everywhere and with everyone, even when doing so meant extreme hardship. What motivated him? Personal gratitude.

In his own words: "The grace of our Lord was poured out on me abundantly, along with the faith and love that are in Christ Jesus. Here is a trustworthy saying that deserves full acceptance: Christ Jesus came into the world to save sinners—of whom I am the worst," 1 Timothy 1:14-15.

We were that lost sheep. We were that lost coin. We were that lost son. True gospel outreach begins with personal gratitude for the fact that Jesus Christ found and redeemed us.

MIRROR, MIRROR

James 1:17-27

In James 1:17-27 the apostle likens God's word to a mirror. "Anyone who listens to the word but does not do what it says is like a man who looks at his face in a mirror..." How is the Bible like a mirror? It reflects. When we look intently into its words, we see ourselves, our world, our relationships, indeed, our EVERYTHING, as God sees them.

It's possible to look into an ordinary mirror and think, "Perfection! I'm really something. I'm well dressed, well liked, well off, and well on my way to great success. I have no need for God in my life."

The Christians in Laodicea thought much the same. They were prosperous, powerful, and popular. They had no need for help from God, and told Him so. Yet, had they looked intently into God's mirror, the Scriptures, they would have seen a different reflection—a reflection Jesus described, saying, "You do not realize that you are wretched, pitiful, poor, blind and naked," Revelation 3:17.

In Scripture God says, "Be holy, because I, the LORD your God, am holy," Leviticus 19:2. He says, "Love the LORD your God with all your heart and with all your soul and with all your strength and with all your mind," Luke 10:27. When we look intently and believingly into the mirror of God's law, can anyone of us claim to be without sin? No.

But how different we look when we see ourselves reflected in the gospel of Christ—the gospel which proclaims, "Therefore, there is now no condemnation for those who are in Christ Jesus," Romans 8:1. When we are in Christ by faith, God no longer sees us as wretched, poor, pitiful, blind, and naked, but as redeemed, restored, forgiven, and well-dressed in the robes of Christ's righteousness.

If you, like so many people, struggle with poor self-image; if you look in an ordinary mirror, thinking, "I'm unattractive, unloved, unwanted;" go to the mirror of God's word and see how you really look to God through Jesus Christ. You aren't unattractive.

In God's eyes, you are radiantly beautiful—as Paul wrote of the entire Christian Church: "...as Christ loved the church and gave Himself up for her to make her holy, cleansing her by the washing with water through the word, and to present her to Himself as a radiant church, without stain or wrinkle or any other blemish, but holy and blameless," Ephesians 5:25-27.

Go to the mirror of God's word, and see how much you are loved—enough for Jesus Christ to offer up His life for you. Go to the mirror of God's word and see how much you are wanted. James wrote that God "chose to give us birth through the word of truth, that we might be a kind of

128

first-fruits of all He created," James 1:18. If God chose you, God wanted you.

If you and I look intently into the mirror of Scripture— the Greek word, PARA-KUPTO, means 'to bend down and inspect,' and is used in the New Testament to describe the manner in which Peter, John, and Mary Magdalene bent over to carefully inspect Christ's empty tomb—we will see how lost we were without Christ, and how saved we are through Christ. This is the image of ourselves we truly need to remember.

Conversely, if we do not see the need to love others as God has loved us; to forgive others as God has forgiven us; to share the truth of Scripture with others as God has shared it with us; perhaps we've forgotten how we look.

Perhaps we need to look more closely at ourselves in God's mirror.

MORE THAN CONQUERORS

Romans 8:31-39

In Romans 8:37 Paul writes: "In all these things we are more than conquerors through Him who loved us." Beautiful, powerful words, aren't they? Only, how many of us look and feel like conquerors?

When I look into a mirror, I don't see a conqueror. I see a middle-aged man with wrinkles, bifocals, and thinning hair. How can I be more than a conqueror if I'm lying in a hospital bed or struggling to pay bills or need a walker to cross the living room?

The answer lies in the last five words of Romans 8:37, "through Him who loved us." We are more than conquerors because God does the conquering. To live life in that sense of overwhelming victory, we need only ask the questions Paul asks and answers in Romans 8:31-39.

If God is for Me, Who can be Against Me?'
The emphasis of this question is not on the "if" but on "God." "If *God* is for us, who can be against us?" Nor is this a multiple-choice question. If God is the God Scripture declares Him to be—all powerful, all knowing, always present; eternal, unchanging, reliable, truthful, and full of grace and compassion—then "who can be against us?" can have only one answer: No one.

No matter what problems you may be facing today, whether physical, financial, emotional, spiritual, or marital, ask yourself: "Are any of my problems more powerful than God?" Because almighty God *is* for you, nothing can defeat you. In Greek, the phrase "who can be against us" is more literally "who is against us." With God on our side, it's as if the opposition does not even exist.

If God Gave Me His own Son, will He not Give Me Everything else I Need?

As Christians, we have no doubt that God has the power to help us. But does He have the willingness? When our problems are not resolved according to our timeframe and specifications, we often think "God doesn't care" or "God is busy elsewhere" or "God has better things to do."

Unfortunately, if we don't believe that God is willing to exercise His power on our behalf, we cannot live like "more than conquerors." Then we will see ourselves as lost and alone in a world filled with trouble and chaos. However, in Romans 8, Paul offers the supreme, indisputable, undeniable, and irrevocable proof of God's willingness to help us. What is it? The cross of Jesus Christ.

If you ever doubt God's willingness to help you, look at the cross of Jesus. Ask yourself: "If God gave the life of His one and only Son to redeem me, will He refuse to help me with anything else?" The answer is no.

If God Justifies Me, Who can Condemn Me?

Few things make us feel less like conquerors than the glaring knowledge of our own sin and guilt. "Why was I so mean and hurtful? Why did I use such language? Why did I surrender to that temptation? Why did I turn away from that person in desperate need?"

The apostle Paul hardly sounds like a conqueror when he laments in Romans 7: "I have the desire to do what is good, but I cannot carry it out. For what I do is not the good I want to do; no, the evil I do not want to do—this I keep on doing . . . What a wretched man I am. Who will rescue me from this body of death?"

But how does he continue? Not with a moan of defeat but a cry of overwhelming victory: "Thanks be to God— through Jesus Christ our Lord!" That we sin, yes. That we deserve only punishment, yes. But here too we are "more than conquerors" through Jesus Christ, who not only died for us; who not only rose again for us; but who is even now interceding for us at the right hand of God.

If God Loves Me, Who can Separate Me from that Love?
When Paul asks, "Who shall separate us from the love of Christ?" he is not talking about our love for Christ but Christ's love for us. Who or what can separate us from that love? Life or death? Height or depth? Good times or bad? The fury of hell itself? Again, the answer is no.

Nothing in all creation can "separate us from the love of God that is in Christ Jesus our Lord." Understand what this means. It means that we are not only eternally safe in the love of Christ. It means that even when we face trying circumstances, Christ still loves us. Christ will always love us. And this is what makes us "more than conquerors."

What Then Shall We Say in Response to This?

I've saved the first question Paul asked for last. It is both an introduction and a conclusion. When Paul posed this question, he may have been referring to the preceding verses of Romans 8 or the preceding chapters of Romans itself. But in a real sense, you and I ask this question daily.

Every day we face new or existing problems. And every problem forces us to ask, "How will I respond to this?" Will I wave the white flag of surrender? Will I drag myself through the day, acting as if I have no hope and no Savior? Or will I press on triumphantly in the promise of Scripture: "In all these things we are more than conquerors through Him who loved us?"

Remember, in Romans 8 Paul is not telling us how to become conquerors. He's telling us to live like the "more than conquerors" we already are in Jesus Christ.

OUT OF THE DEPTHS

Psalm 130

All of us have been "in the depths." We may have used other expressions like "I feel so low" or "I'm stuck in a rut" or "I'm down in the dumps," but the meaning is the same. At times this type of depression and disappointment can seem like an abyss. In fact, the Hebrew word translated as "depths" in Psalm 130:1 is also used to describe the depths of the ocean in Isaiah 51:10. But if the writer of Psalm 130 knew what it was like to be "in the depths," he also knew the way out: prayer, forgiveness, and patience.

When Down, Look Up

When the writer of Psalm 130 found himself in deep trouble and despair, he brought his burdens to the LORD—to Jehovah, the eternal "I AM;" a name for God that appears nearly seven hundred times in the Psalms, and perhaps the one name of God more than any other that emphasizes the lasting nature of His faithfulness. He is always with us in our peaks and valleys, in our ups and downs.

"Out of the depths I cry to you, O LORD," said the psalmist. The Hebrew verb he used means to cry out loudly and at times even wordlessly. For the child of God, sobs and moans and groans are prayers too; prayers understood and acted upon by the Almighty.

Of course, when we are feeling low, it's easy to give up on prayer. It's easy to think, "What's the point? God isn't listening anyway." On occasion, the psalmists felt this way too. David wrote in Psalm 27: "Do not hide Your face from me, do not turn Your servant away in anger; You have been my helper. Do not reject me or forsake me, O God my Savior." But God is listening. We have His promise: "Call upon Me in the day of trouble; I will deliver you, and you will honor Me," Psalm 50:15.

When feeling down, how vital that we look up to God in prayer. Prayer is not for God's sake but for our sakes. It keeps our faith focused on God instead of ourselves, and teaches us to rely on God's strength and wisdom instead of our own.

This is not vain theological thinking or locker-room pep-talk. This is divine truth. The connection between giving our burdens to God and obtaining peace of mind is clearly established in Philippians 4:6-7: "Do not be anxious about anything, but in everything, by prayer and petition, with thanksgiving, present your requests to God. And the peace of God, which transcends all understanding, will guard your hearts and minds in Christ Jesus."

Trust in God's Grace, Compassion, and Forgiveness
Often we find ourselves "in the depths" because of a spiritual crisis; because we feel the terrible weight of sin and guilt and find it hard to believe that God, even our merciful God, would ever forgive us. Imagine what would happen if God did keep a record of our wrongs. Imagine coming to

135

God with a burden of sin and hearing Him say, "Oh no, not *you* again. (SIGH.) Well, let Me check the record-book."

Yet, Psalm 130 declares of God: "But with You there is forgiveness; therefore are You feared," Psalm 130:4. Through God's grace, compassion, and forgiveness in Jesus Christ, we can be certain that God will always be attentive to our prayers and always deliver us from the horrible pit of our despair and problems.

Wait for the Lord to Lift You Up
Even in the best of times, waiting for the Lord to act or answer can be difficult. But in the worst of times, when we find ourselves in deep trouble (as was the writer of Psalm 130), waiting for God may seem all but impossible. Long days and sleepless nights can become fertile seeds of doubt, which grow into nagging questions like "Where is God?" and "If God cared, would He make me wait?"

Yet, amid all his fears and troubles the psalmist declared, "I wait for the LORD, my soul waits," Psalm 130:5. The Hebrew word he used, KAVAH, like many Bible words for "wait," contains the idea of strength and patience; not just the strength and patience needed to wait, but the strength and patience waiting produces. The psalmist was willing to wait for the LORD because he fully expected the faithful "I AM" to deliver him. His hopeful expectation was the same as the watchmen who waited for the first gray sliver of dawn and the new day certain to follow.

Where does this hope originate? The psalmist tells us this too: "In His word I put my hope," Psalm 130:5; the only word in heaven and on earth that will never disappoint us. If you find yourself "in the depths" of trouble or despair, be confident that God will deliver you.

Just wait. You'll see.

OVERCOMING LOW SELF-ESTEEM

Psalm 130

People with low self-esteem feel worthless. They continually say things like "I'm a failure. I can't do anything right." Dismal expressions like these often become self-fulfilling prophecies. Those who expect to fail usually do fail. And with each failure, low self-esteem sinks even lower.

Many factors can contribute to low self-esteem: relationships, divorce, past experiences, other people, especially parents. The apostle Paul wrote in Ephesians 6:4, "Fathers, do not exasperate your children; instead, bring them up in the training and instruction of the Lord." But many children grow up in homes where they are unloved, unwanted, and ridiculed. "You're worthless. You'll never amount to anything. You should have never been born." What view of self and the world will such children have?

Low self-esteem can lead to self-destructive behavior, including alcoholism, drug abuse, eating disorders, promiscuity, being hyper-critical of others, and an increased risk of suicide. All of these actions are merely attempts to conceal or compensate for a sense of worthlessness. If you are struggling with low self-esteem, consider the following:

You were Made by God and for God

Paul wrote in Colossians 1:16, "All things were made through Him and for Him." This is why all the fame, fortune, power, and possessions in the world cannot provide lasting happiness or genuine self-esteem. You were created for God; and only in God can you find purpose and worth.

You are a Unique Creation of God

Since the beginning of time, God has made billions of people; but He only made one you. You are as unique as your fingerprints, retina pattern, and DNA. God didn't have to make you. God *wanted* to make you—wanted you here at this time, this place, with these opportunities. Do you realize how special you should feel?

You are Dearly Loved by God

Few things can make one feel more worthless than feeling unloved. Even at a purely human level, saying "I love you" is like pouring water on a thirsty, dying plant. It makes us grow, thrive, and blossom. But while human love can fade and fail, God's love for you cannot. His love is eternal and unchanging. And He has proven His love in the sacrifice of His Son, Jesus Christ. "But God demonstrates His own love for us in this: While we were still sinners, Christ died for us," Romans 5:8.

You are of Immeasurable Worth to God

The value of something is determined by its purchase price. God purchased—redeemed, literally meaning 'to buy back'—you through the priceless blood of Christ. Do you see how much He values you? The apostle Peter wrote:

"For you know that it was not with perishable things such as silver or gold that you were redeemed from the empty way of life handed down to you from your forefathers, but with the precious blood of Christ, a lamb without blemish or defect," 1 Peter 1:18-19.

You were Chosen by God

Others may look past you, underestimate you, laugh at your accomplishments, or pick you last for the team. But God chose you in eternity to be one of His own. Paul told the Christians at Rome: "For you did not receive a spirit that makes you a slave again to fear, but you received the Spirit of sonship," Roman 8:15. In this verse "sonship" literally means "adoption." God adopted you, brought you to faith, gave you the family name and inheritance because He wanted you.

PACK YOUR SUITCASE, SON

Romans 8:14-17

I'm adopted.

On June 12, 1953, after I'd spent two and a half months in an orphanage in Tampa, Florida, my new parents, Paul and Carol Weis, took me home. On the day this happened, my dad looked at me, smiled, and said, "Pack your suitcase, son. We're going home."

I've often contemplated what this selfless, loving act of adoption brought to me: a name, a home, an inheritance, and a family. I can particularly identify with the words of Paul in Romans 8:15, "You received the Spirit of sonship." The Greek word translated as sonship literally means 'to place as a son;' in other words, 'to adopt.'

Adopted by God's Grace

I did not choose my adoptive parents; they chose me. My only "contribution" was to lie in my crib, wide-eyed, slobber-mouthed, and wearing a messy diaper.

In a similar way, we did not choose God; God chose us. Paul wrote in Ephesians 1:4, "He chose us in Him before the creation of the world to be holy and blameless in His sight." That God chose you means He wanted you. Your faith is no accident. Think of the impact on your life, career, marriage, ministry, or self-esteem if you got up every morning saying,

141

"God chose me. God wanted me. I am not a child of destiny; I am a child of God."

A Father in Heaven

Few people have had more of a profound impact on my life than my father. His love, guidance, and encouragement were constant since the day he said, "Pack your suitcase, son. We're going home." In him I truly glimpsed the meaning of having a Father in heaven.

Jesus taught us to pray in view of this same endearing, familiar, and trusting relationship, saying, "Our Father who art in heaven." What a difference this should make to our prayers and expectations.

You Look Just Like Your Dad

Over the years people have told me, "You look just like your dad." How can this be when I was adopted? I don't know.

But then, shouldn't we as the adopted children of God grow more and more to look like our Father in heaven—not in appearance, of course, but in behavior, language, lifestyle, priorities, and choices. Isn't this what Paul meant when he wrote in Ephesians 5:1, "Be imitators of God, therefore, as dearly loved children?" Can others look at us and see the Family resemblance?

Pack Your Suitcase, Son; We're Going Home

For me this phrase has always summarized every blessing that came to me through adoption. In a sense,

God said the same to you when He adopted you into His Family. And when the time comes for us to leave this earth and claim our heavenly inheritance, I suspect we'll hear a similar phrase: "Pack your suitcase, My child. It is time to go home."

PARABLE OF THE MINAS

Luke 19:11-27

When Jesus told the *Parable of the Minas*, He was nearing the end of His final journey from Galilee to Jerusalem. Ahead lay the agonies of His passion: Betrayal, beatings, mockery, blood, crucifixion. Yet, as Luke tells us in his gospel record, Jesus made this final journey resolutely and willingly. In fact, He Himself was leading the way.

Only seventeen miles from Jerusalem, Jesus passed through Jericho, where He healed blind Bartimaeus and visited the home of Zacchaeus the tax collector. When the people of Jericho saw this miracle, they rejoiced and praised God. But when they saw Jesus go to the home of a tax collector, they grumbled, saying, "He has gone to be the guest of a sinner."

In other words, they wanted a Messiah who could work miracles, but not a Messiah who saved sinners. They wrongly concluded that Jesus was traveling to Jerusalem to claim an earthly kingship and visible kingdom. And who better to have in political office than one who could work miracles—heal the sick, raise the dead, win wars, defeat the hated Romans, and feed thousands from five small barley loaves and two small fish?

Yet, like so many then and now, the people of Jericho were completely wrong in their assessment of the person

144

and work of the Messiah and the true nature of His kingdom. Jesus told the *Parable of the Minas* to correct these misconceptions, as Luke explains in 19:11, "While they were listening to this, He went on to tell them a parable, because He was near Jerusalem and the people thought that the kingdom of God was going to appear at once."

In the *Parable of the Minas* a nobleman travels to a distant country to receive a kingdom. Before leaving, he gives his servants a mina—currency worth about three months' wages at the time of Jesus—and tells them to "conduct business" in his absence.

Because his destination is far away, he is gone for a long while. But when the nobleman returns, he is a king with a visible kingdom. He destroys all those citizens who rejected his rule, and then requires an accounting of how his servants used their minas. Of the three servants interviewed, two are commended for their profitable activity; one is rebuked for doing nothing.

And the deeper meaning of the parable? Jesus is the nobleman. After completing the work of our salvation, He traveled to the "far-away country" of heaven to receive His kingdom.

Contrary to the expectations of the people in Jericho, that kingdom and its King will only become visible at the end of time, when Jesus returns to judge the living and the dead. For believers His return is one of joyful anticipation, for we will see the King of Kings in His glory and the now invisible kingdom of God in its fullness. But for the unbelieving—those who, as in the parable, declared, "We don't want this man to be our king"— the return of Jesus will spell disaster and destruction. A dreadful thought, but nonetheless true.

As the nobleman in the parable gave minas to his servants, so the ascended Lord has given "minas" or gifts to each one of us for supporting the gospel ministry—that precious message which builds the kingdom of God in human hearts: "The Son of Man came to seek and to save what was lost," Luke 19:10.

Our individual minas vary, but they are all of equal value to the Lord. We may never see visible results as we use our minas. But from the perspective of our noble King, the most import thing is the ongoing faithfulness of our investment. When He returns, may we all hear the welcome words, "Well done, my good servant!"

PATIENCE AMID SUFFERING

James 5:7-11

The epistle of James was written in part to comfort persecuted Christians. It opens with the words: "Consider it pure joy, my brothers, whenever you face trials of many kinds, because you know that the testing of your faith develops perseverance. Perseverance must finish its work so that you may be mature and complete, not lacking anything." In 5:7-11 James offers four imperatives for obtaining patience amid suffering.

Live Life in the Certainty of Christ's Second Coming
Notice that in 5:7 James speaks of the Lord's coming with absolutely certainty. So does the entire New Testament; and to such an extent that twenty-four of the twenty-seven books in the New Testament reference the second coming of Jesus. It's this certainty that gives us such patience amid suffering. For we know that when the Lord returns, He will right every wrong, wipe away every tear, and give us glorified bodies like His own.

This certainty moved the apostle Paul to write: "I consider that our present sufferings are not worth comparing with the glory that will be revealed in us." This certainty also restructures our lives, choices, and priorities. It makes us ask ourselves, "So, how important is money to my future happiness? Why do I have to get so impatient with other people?" The certainty of Christ's return empowers us to be patient and slow to anger.

Stand Firm Because the Lord's Coming is Near

It's not only the certainty of Christ's return that give us patience; it is also the nearness of His return. "Jesus will be here soon" is welcome news to anyone who is suffering. Yet, while James is referring primarily to the PAROUSIA or second coming of Christ, God comes near us *now* in other ways.

God is near us in our trouble. Scripture says that "the LORD is near to all who call on Him." God is near us in our humanity. This is the lesson of Christmas and the Incarnation. Jesus came to be with us and one of us. And for this reason the letter to the Hebrews declares: "We do not have a high priest who is unable to sympathize with our weaknesses, but we have one who has been tempted in every way, just as we are—yet was without sin. Let us then approach the throne of grace with confidence, so that we may receive mercy and find grace to help in our time of need."

And God is always near us in His word, the Bible. It's the nearness of God that enables us to "stand firm," as James says in 5:8, and to say, "No, I refuse to surrender to my problems."

Don't Grumble, for the Judge is at the Door

James reminds us again of the imminence of the Lord's return in 5:9; but this time for a more sobering reason:

Judgment. He writes: "Don't grumble against each other, brothers, or you will be judged. The Judge is standing at the door."

This imperative of James is not so much a call to patience as it is a warning against impatience. For it is when we are impatient with others—spouses, children, friends, strangers, fellow Christians, even God Himself—that we tend to grumble. Need a reason not to be impatient? Consider this: If God were impatient with us, what would our fate be?

Consider the Lessons Learned from Suffering

In calling us to patience James asks us to consider the sufferings and patience of the Old Testament prophets and the perseverance of Job. If you've read about Job, then you know that this man of God suffered enormous tragedy. One day his life was good. The next day he lost nearly everything: Children, wealth, property, possessions, servants, livestock, prestige, and finally his health.

Yet, James reminds us not only of Job's suffering but the God-appointed end of it. The book of Job ends with the words: "The LORD blessed the latter part of Job's life more than the first."

Certainly, none of us enjoy suffering. None of us want problems. But when we go through difficult times, we know that the end of each struggle will be the same end God brought about for Job; namely, our lives will be doubly blessed.

The greatest lesson we learn from suffering is the lesson with which James closes this text: "The Lord is full of compassion and mercy."

REFUGE

Psalm 46

Many people seek refuge in all the wrong places. But because God is our refuge and strength, we can confidently say, "'We will not fear—anything."

God's Strength at Work in Our Lives

Psalm 46:1-3 describes a scene of chaos and upheaval: the earth removed; mountains cast into the sea; waters roaring and troubled. This may well refer to a cataclysmic event in nature; or, the images may symbolize the chaos and upheaval of life.

The phrase "though the earth be removed" is more literally "though the earth be changed." And for human beings, few things are more frightening than change. Yet, Scripture assures us that God never changes. "I the LORD do not change," Malachi 3:6. This means that God does not love us today and hate us tomorrow. He is not for us one day and against us the next. Instead, as Psalm 46 declares, He remains a "very *present* help in trouble"

Sadly, many people seek refuge in all the wrong places: fame, fortune, careers, even addictions. Each of these refuges are doomed to fail. But God never fails. And this is why the first word of Psalm 46 is one of its most important words: "*God* is our refuge and strength."

The Hebrew for God throughout Psalm 46 is ELOHIM. ELOHIM is actually a plural word; not in the sense of 'many gods,' but rather 'fullness.' Fullness of grace. Fullness of wisdom. Fullness of love, mercy, and power. And this is why—*God* is why—we can confidently say: "We will not fear." We will not fear sickness. We will not fear death. We will not fear what others say about us. We will not fear terrorist attacks. We will not fear anything.

God's Personal Involvement in Our Lives

If Psalm 46:1-3 assures us of God's power at work in our lives, then Psalm 46:4-7 assures us of God's personal involvement in our lives. And these two important facts— God's power and willingness—are addressed in verses 7 and 11 of this psalm. God is not only called the "LORD of Armies;" He is also called the "God of Jacob." He is God over all, but also the God of the individual.

God is in our midst. God is on our side. These are the constant refrains of Scripture, and loudly heralded in Psalm 46: "God is in the midst of her; she shall not be moved. God shall help her, just at the break of dawn." And where do we see God more in our midst and more on our side than in the coming of our Savior, Jesus Christ? Clearly, God has the power and willingness to help us.

God's Selah

Psalm 46:8-11 comprises the last section of this great psalm. Much could be said about these verses. In an age of wars and rumors of wars, terrorist threats, the boasts and swagger of nations and leaders, how comforting to remember that GOD IS IN CONTROL. "He makes wars to cease. He breaks the bow and cuts the spear in two. He burns the chariots in the fire."

Notice particularly Psalm 46:10. In this verse God turns to us directly and says, "Be still and know that I am God." This is the one SELAH from Psalm 46—SELAH is a Hebrew word meaning to stop, be silent, and reflect—that we need to remember most of all. When overloaded by life's worries, anxieties, and burdens, we need to stop, be silent, listen, and reflect on what God is saying. He's saying, "I am God. You are not."

There is no better, no safer refuge.

REST FOR THE WEARY

Matthew 11:25-30

Laboring and Heavy Laden

Labor means hard work. Heavy laden means weighed down. It's instructive to see how the Bible uses these two words in other settings. For example, Luke 5:5 uses the word *labor* to describe how the disciples struggled all night without catching a single fish. They rowed. They lowered and raised their nets. They grew increasingly weary and frustrated. But the same may happen to us when we labor to save a troubled marriage, beat an addiction, find a job, or resist temptation.

Acts 27:10 uses the words *heavy laden* to describe the cargo of a ship. Don't we often carry our problems like heavy cargo, sinking deeper and deeper into doubt and despair? Jesus used the same words to describe how Israel's religious leaders were burdening people with made-up additions to the Mosaic Law, saying, "You load people down with heavy burdens they can hardly carry, and you yourselves will not lift a finger to help them," Luke 11:46.

Rest for Soul and Body

In Matthew 11:29 Jesus says, "And you will find rest for your souls"—that deep, inner part of our being that cannot be reached or rejuvenated by Ambien or eight hours of uninterrupted sleep; but can only be satisfied and set at rest by Jesus Christ. The psalmist did not say, 'My soul thirsts

154

for Gatorade.' He said, "My soul thirsts for God, for the living God," Psalm 42:2.

Yet, while the emphasis of Matthew 11:25-30 is on spiritual rest, surely bodily rest is included too. Bodily rest is intimately connected to spiritual rest. If we are tossing and turning on the inside, we are usually tossing and turning in our beds.

I'm not suggesting that turning to Jesus is a magic cure for insomnia. But I am suggesting that if we truly gave our worries and burdens to God instead of chewing on them like worn-out, tasteless gum, we would sleep better at night. The psalmist apparently felt the same, saying, "I will lie down and sleep in peace, because You alone, O LORD, make me dwell in safety," Psalm 4:8.

The Imperatives of Rest

Rest is imperative. In Matthew 11:25-30 Jesus uses three imperative verbs to teach us where to find rest and how to stay rested. The first imperative is "come to Me," Matthew 11:28. Why come to Jesus for rest? No one else can provide it. Any other means of finding rest—fame, fortune, career, relationships, narcotics, alcohol, the recommendations of the Wise and Prudent—are temporary at best and destructive at worst. Type "How to Find Inner Peace" into an internet search engine, you'll find millions of different websites with differing answers. The Bible offers only one answer. If you want true rest, turn to Jesus Christ.

The second imperative is "take My yoke," Matthew 11:29. If "come" is a verb of invitation, "take" is a verb of application. We know where to find answers—the Bible; but we often struggle to apply them. We hear the invitation of Jesus, "Come to Me," but we don't always come. Why?

At times, we may view the Bible as small and insignificant when compared to our labors and burdens; as if Jesus were fine for Sunday school and little children, but not adults living in a grown-up world of wars, terrorism, disease, death, bankruptcies, and foreclosures.

Yet, this was the very 'grown-up' pretentiousness Jesus opposed when He said, "I thank You, Father, Lord of heaven and earth, that You have hidden these things from the wise and prudent and have revealed them to babes," Matthew 11:25. The Greek word translated as "babe" can also mean "childlike." And it is when we turn to Jesus in childlike faith that we find rest.

The third imperative of Jesus is "learn from Me," Matthew 11:29. Nothing robs us of sound sleep more than uncertainty—all the *what if* questions: What if I get sick? What if I die? What if I lose my job? What if I can't pay my bills? The list is endless. And at the heart of this list is the all-too-frequent assumption that God does not care about our labors and burdens. This is why Jesus said, "Learn from Me."

As we learn more and more about Jesus, we see how much God loves us and what God was willing to sacrifice to save us.

And in this knowledge we find true rest.

SELFISHNESS OR SERVICE?

Matthew 20:17-28

The cross of Jesus is at the heart of Christian behavior. When God teaches us to forgive, He does so in view of the cross. "Be kind and compassionate to one another, forgiving each other, just as in Christ God forgave you. Be imitators of God, therefore, as dearly loved children and live a life of love, just as Christ loved us and gave Himself up for us as a fragrant offering and sacrifice to God," Ephesians 4:32ff.

The same is true of marriage, Ephesians 5:23; our response to injustice, 1 Peter 2:21-24; the encouragement to be cheerful givers—the Greek word for cheerful is HILAROS, the source of our English word hilarious, 2 Corinthians 8:9; and the call to display gentleness and humility, Philippians 2:4-8.

Everything looks vastly different when viewed through the cross of Jesus: Sin and forgiveness, works and grace, marriage and ministry, poverty and wealth, sickness and health, loneliness and togetherness. And this is certainly true of selfish ambition versus selfless service.

An Unobstructed View of the Cross
Matthew 20:17-28 opens with an unobstructed view of the cross: "Now as Jesus was going up to Jerusalem, He took the twelve disciples aside and said to them, 'We are going up to Jerusalem, and the Son of Man will be betrayed to the

chief priests and the teachers of the law. They will condemn Him to death and will turn Him over to the Gentiles to be mocked and flogged and crucified. On the third day He will be raised to life," Matthew 20:17-19.

This was actually the third such prediction Jesus gave of His impending death. The first occurred in Matthew 16:21 and the second in Matthew 17:22-23. Consider the details Jesus provided His disciples with these three predictions: Betrayal; direct involvement by the religious leaders, elders, Jews and Gentiles; a trial followed by condemnation, mocking, flogging, and crucifixion; execution in Jerusalem; and finally the certainty of His resurrection.

With all of these details in view, I don't know which is more remarkable; that Luke should write in his gospel, "The disciples did not understand any of this;" or that Jesus Christ, knowing full well what agonies lay ahead, should nevertheless walk unswervingly and determinedly to the cross. Scripture states so simply, "Carrying His own cross, He went out to the place of the Skull (which in Aramaic is called Golgotha). Here they crucified Him," John 19:17-18.

Amid our busy, hectic lives, do we still appreciate the significance of these words? Is the cross as firmly grounded in our hearts as it was on Calvary? Do we understand the agonies Jesus endured to redeem us; not just the physical torture—mocking, spitting, beating, flogging; the nails in wrists and feet; in all likelihood, dislocated shoulders, elbows, and wrists; the constant struggle to breath and the shame of being crucified naked—but more unimaginable still, the weight of the world's sin and guilt on His divine shoulders?

Several years ago, as I was nonchalantly flipping between TV channels, I stumbled upon a documentary about crucifixion produced by a medical doctor. When it was over, I found myself weeping. I whispered through a choked voice, "Oh, Lord Jesus, how could we have done that to You? How could You have endured that for us?"

In View of the Cross: Selfishness or Service?
When viewed through the cross of Jesus, the request of James and John in Matthew 20 and the indignant response of the other ten disciples seem rather petty—more self-serving than service-minded. While it is easy for us to berate them, it is always important to examine motives, even religious motives, in view of the cross.

When the size of a congregation is more important than preaching the word of God in its fullness, this is selfishness, not service. When building plans are more important than building people up in the faith, this is selfishness, not service. When hearing "Great sermon, Pastor!" is more important than glorifying the name of God, this is selfishness, not service. "Not so with you," said Jesus. Selfishness and selfish ambition have no place among God's people. Why?

By God's grace we have come to recognize Jesus Christ as our Lord and Savior; the one who selflessly gave His own life as a ransom—the Greek word is LUTRON; the price paid in order to buy a slave's freedom—for the sins of the world. When we know and believe this, how can we be selfish?

Only hours before His crucifixion, Jesus Christ, the Son of God and Creator of the universe, got down on His hands and knees and washed the filthy feet of His disciples. Afterwards, He asked them a question. "Do you understand what I have done for you? You call me 'Teacher' and 'Lord,' and rightly so, for that is what I am. Now that I, your Lord and Teacher, have washed your feet, you also should wash one another's feet. I have set you an example that you should do as I have done for you," John 13:12-15.

What has Jesus done for you? Answer this question and you will have no problem choosing between selfish ambition and selfless service.

SLEEP

Psalm 4

Amid an armed rebellion and with his life in danger, David was still able to find peaceful sleep. How? Psalm 4 provides the answer.

David Prayed

David found the peace to sleep by giving his problems to the Lord in prayer. He knew that God would hear and answer, because God was the source of his eternal salvation and God had never failed him in the past. We too give our problems to the Lord. Unfortunately, we don't always leave them there. Instead, worrying that God won't hear, answer, or act, we snatch our problems back, struggling to carry what only God can. And still we wonder why we can't sleep.

When sleepless, our prayer should be similar to David's. "O Lord, in undeserved grace You saved me when I could not save myself. Looking back on my life, I cannot name one time when You failed me. And I know You will not fail me in my current distress."

A millennia after David, the apostle Paul made this same declaration in Romans 8:32, saying, "He who did not spare His own Son, but gave Him up for us all—how will He not also, along with Him, graciously give us all things?" The point is, if God loved you enough to give you Jesus Christ, will He refuse to give you a loaf of bread, change of clothes, place to shelter, or the means to repair a troubled marriage? No. Give your problems to God and leave them with God. You'll sleep in peace.

David Weighed

David also found sleep by weighing his enemies against God's infinite love and power. In the privacy of his thoughts he called out the opposition and asked, "Who are you when compared to God?" When sleepless, we should weigh our opposition in the same way. "Financial trouble, who do you think you are? Sickness, who do you think you are? Loneliness, who do you think you are?" You are nothing compared to the God who loves me, hears me when I call, and has set me apart as His very own.

In Romans 8:31 Paul invited this same comparison. He asked, "What, then, shall we say in response to this? If God is for us, who can be against us?" So, what's *your* answer? If your answer is "no one and nothing," turn out the light and go to sleep.

David Stayed

Few things cause more agitation and sleeplessness than anger. When angry, we can't sleep. Instead, we toss and turn. We roam through the house at 2:00 A.M., bath-robed and bleary-eyed, nursing our injuries and anger, and saying things like "I can't believe she embarrassed me that way! I can't believe he treated me so badly after so many years of marriage!"

However, rather than to nurse his anger, David stayed his heart, mind, and faith on the word of God. Instead of plotting revenge on those who betrayed him, he stayed in his bed, quietly meditating on how God would want him to behave—referred to in Psalm 4:5 as the "sacrifices of righteousness."

And yes, at times, doing the right thing requires sacrifice. But for David the antidote to angry sleeplessness was to "put your trust in the LORD." Said another way, if anger is keeping you up at night, don't take matters into your hands, place them into God's hands. Instead of counting sheep, count on the Good Shepherd.

David Laid

Through prayer, through weighing his problems, through staying his mind and heart on the Scriptures, David was able to lay his problems to rest and his head on his pillow. While others were saying, "Who will show us any good?" Psalm 4:6, David expected only the best from God.

Using words reminiscent of the Aaronic Benediction, David said, "LORD, lift up the light of Your countenance upon us." And dear friend, if you go to bed each night knowing that almighty God is smiling on you in the fullness and brightness of His grace, you will sleep in peace.

STOP CRYING, START LIVING

Luke 7:11-17

Tears are a part of life. Young or old, male or female, we all cry. Tears are so much a part of our lives that over our lifetime we will cry an average of twenty-one gallons of tears. Of course, not all tears are sad tears. There are tears of joy too. But given the sinful world we live in, most of our tears are sad tears. Tears of remorse and loss. Tears of grief and guilt. Tears of frustration and failure.

The widow of Nain was crying too. How tragic her life had been! First her husband had died, and then her only son. It's easy to imagine her dressed in black and bent with grief, her eyes red and swollen from crying.

It's also easy to imagine her questions: "Why did God let this happen? Does He know what I'm going through? Does He care?" In grief or loss we've all asked similar questions. And yet, how little did that widow know that when Jesus stopped the funeral procession at Nain City Limits, God Himself was standing mere inches from her need and sorrow.

When we feel as if God is unaware of our problems, we should hurry to Nain and remember this widow. We don't know her name. We don't know the name of her deceased husband or dead son. All we do know is that she'd been heartbroken by tragedy and that she lived in a small town.

In fact, everything about Luke 7:11-17 screams "SMALL" and "INSIGNIFICANT" and "DON'T BOTHER STOPPING HERE." And yet, where do we find God? In Nain. It may well be that Jesus Christ, God the Son, went to the small, insignificant town of Nain to dry the tears of one small and insignificant widow.

Never doubt that God sees our tears too. He does. He knows us inside and out, as the Psalmist wrote: "O LORD, You have searched me and You know me." He knows the number of hairs on our head and the number of tears in our eyes. And those tears always move Him to compassion.

When Jesus saw the widow of Nain crying, His heart went out to her—God's infinitely loving and merciful heart. When Jesus wept at the funeral of His friend Lazarus, God was weeping. When Jesus wept over Jerusalem, God was weeping. When Jesus cried tears of blood in Gethsemane, God was weeping.

God sees our tears. God feels our pain. These are two of the three great lessons of Nain. And the third lesson? To that poor widow Jesus said, "Stop crying." And she did. Then to the corpse in the coffin Jesus said, "Start living." And he did.

The very same word of the very same God dries our sad tears and empowers us to move on with our lives. And it is the same word that will at the end of time call the dead from their graves and give all believers in Christ glorified resurrection bodies—and eyes that will never again cry a single sad tear.

TEMPTED IN THE WILDERNESS

Matthew 4:1-11

The three temptations recorded in Matthew 4:1-11 were not the only temptations Jesus faced. Luke 4 states that Jesus was tempted throughout His forty days in the wilderness; furthermore, that when the devil finally left Jesus in the wilderness, it was only until a more "opportune time."

Whether desert or city, Gethsemane or Calvary, the devil was always lurking nearby, desperately trying to entice Jesus to sin or to dissuade Him from the cross. Still, there was something especially important about the temptation in the wilderness. It was neither an accident nor a coincidence, but clearly ordained by God. Notice what Matthew 4:1 states: "Then Jesus was *led* by the Spirit into the desert to be tempted by the devil." Who led Jesus? The Holy Spirit. For what specific purpose? To be tempted by the devil. Why?

Why Jesus was Tempted
The Greek word translated as "tempted" in Matthew 4:1 can also mean "tested." Its basic meaning is "to try something out" in order to determine its quality. In essence, both testing and tempting are tests. The real difference lies in their desired outcome. Testing is meant to bring success. Tempting is meant to bring failure. God tests. The devil tempts. By testing, God wants to increase faith. By tempting, the devil wants to destroy it.

The temptation in the wilderness occurred at a crucial time for Jesus. He had just been baptized in the Jordan River. He had seen the Holy Spirit descending upon Him in the form of a dove. He had heard the testimony of God the Father, "This is My Son whom I love; with Him I am well pleased." But before assuming His messianic ministry, He was tested to prove His qualifications and readiness to be our Savior. And oh, how much depended on the outcome of this test!

Jesus was tempted in the wilderness, but the truer context was Eden where, through the devil's temptation, the first Adam had failed the test and brought sin and death into the world. In Scripture Jesus is called the second Adam upon whom the fate of all mankind also rested. Would the second Adam fail the test too? Would He succumb to the temptations of the devil?

Thank God, no. Where the first Adam failed, the second Adam, Jesus Christ—true Man and true God—gloriously succeeded. Paul writes of this in Romans 5:17, "For if, by the trespass of the one man, death reigned through that one man, how much more will those who receive God's abundant provision of grace and of the gift of righteousness reign in life through the one man, Jesus Christ."

How Jesus Was Tempted

The heart of the temptation in Eden was doubt. "Did God really say...?" Doubt was also at the heart of the three temptations recorded in Matthew 4:1-11. When the devil urged Jesus to turn stones into bread, he was really saying: "God led You into this wilderness, Jesus, but then abandoned You. You're on Your own and starving. Don't trust in God. Feed Yourself."

When the devil told Jesus to leap down from the temple, he was really saying: "Okay, Jesus, You say You trust in God; so then jump." Do you see the cleverness of this temptation? Under the guise of trust the devil was attempting to create mistrust. Purposely placing oneself in danger is not saying "I trust you, God." It is saying just the opposite: "I don't trust you, God. Prove Yourself to me."

When the devil promised Jesus all the kingdoms of the world in exchange for the Savior's worship, he was really saying: "Jesus, that so-called loving Father of Yours wants You to bleed and die to win the world. I'm offering You a far easier, far less painful way. All of this can be Yours"—think game show host—"if the price is right. Trust me." For Satan, the right price was having the Son of God bow down in worship.

What the Temptation in the Wilderness Means for Us

You and I are tempted by this same devil. His very names describe his malicious intent. In this text alone he is called *Devil*, meaning "slanderer;" *Satan*, meaning "adversary;" and finally the *Tempter*. Elsewhere Scripture calls him *Beelzebub*, meaning "lord of dung;" also *Serpent, Dragon, Murderer, Enemy, Beast, Father of Lies*, and in 1 Peter 5:8, a being who "prowls about like a roaring lion looking for someone to devour." Despite all his years and wiles, his modus operandi remains unchanged. He looks for weaknesses and wildernesses—troubled marriages, financial difficulties, spiritual fatigue, bodily pain.

On our own we cannot defeat the devil, which is precisely why the apostle Paul urges us to "put on the full armor of God so that you can take your stand against the devil's schemes;" and why the apostle Peter tells us to resist the devil, "standing firm in the faith." The devil is a dangerous adversary; but through the righteousness and atoning death of Jesus Christ, the devil is also a *defeated* enemy, who must always flee before the "it is written" of the Scriptures.

What a comforting thing for us to know that when we are tempted by the devil, as Martin Luther said, "one little word can fell him;" even more so, that in Jesus Christ "we do not have a high priest who is unable to sympathize with our weaknesses, but we have one who has been tempted in every way, just as we are—yet was without sin. Let us then approach the throne of grace with confidence, so that we may receive mercy and find grace to help in our time of need," Hebrews 4:15-16.

THE CALL TO DISCIPLESHIP

Matthew 9:9-13

Matthew was one of the Lord's original twelve disciples and apostles, and of course the author of the gospel record bearing his name. However, at least four aspects of Matthew's call to discipleship are identical to our own call.

Discipleship is a Call from God

Matthew 9:9 states: "As Jesus went on from there, He saw a man named Matthew at the tax collector's booth." Who saw Matthew? Jesus did. Who went to Matthew? Jesus did. Who called Matthew? Jesus did. Matthew did not come to Jesus on his own.

While we often hear well-intended talk about a "decision for Christ," humans by nature cannot make this decision. Christians are children of God "born not of natural descent, nor of human decision or of a husband's will, but born of God," John 1:13. Jesus Himself said, "You did not choose Me, but I chose you," John 15:16.

As one who was adopted as an infant, I find these words of Jesus especially meaningful. Being adopted meant I was wanted. And so it is with our adoption into the family of God. Your discipleship is no accident. Jesus chose you. Remember this when you feel alone, worried, helpless, or unwanted.

Remember that the Savior who called you to follow Him will never abandon you or lead you astray. As Paul told the Philippians, "Being confident of this, that He who began a good work in you will carry it on to completion until the day of Christ Jesus," Philippians 1:6.

Discipleship is a Call of Grace

Matthew was a tax collector. Even the modern dislike for taxation and the IRS cannot begin to approximate the hatred and revulsion the Jews felt for men like Matthew. Tax collectors were notorious for greed, fraud, corruption, and even mob-style intimidation. As a Jew collecting taxes for the hated Roman government, Matthew would have also been viewed as a collaborator or traitor by his countrymen.

"Why does your Teacher eat with tax collectors and sinners?" the Pharisees asked. The answer is: Jesus Christ came into the world to save sinners—Matthew, you, me, all sinners. Had Jesus not dined with sinners, He would have always dined alone. Had Jesus not come to save sinners, He would have had no one to save. Discipleship has nothing to do with who we are and everything to do with who God is; the God who said, "I desire mercy, not sacrifice."

Discipleship is a Call for Change

When we travel to one place, we must leave another. The same is true of the call to discipleship. When we follow Jesus by faith, we must be willing to leave other things behind. At the invitation of Jesus, Matthew "arose and followed Him," leaving behind a lucrative business and a dishonest way of life. Why? Why would Matthew leave his tax collector's booth—Peter and Andrew their nets; James and John their father and boat? I'm certain all five of these disciples would say "amen" to the Apostle Paul's explanation: "For whatever was to my profit, I now consider loss for the sake of Christ," Philippians 3:7.

Interestingly, Matthew's name is mentioned in the New Testament books of Matthew, Mark, Luke, and Acts. But only Matthew refers to himself as "Matthew the tax collector." It's as if he never wanted to forget what he had once been, and how the love of Jesus Christ had found, called, saved, and changed him.

Discipleship is a Call to Share
After his call to discipleship, Matthew hosted a dinner in his home for Jesus. Many tax collectors and 'sinners' were in attendance. What made Matthew such an effective witness for Christ? Years in the seminary? No. A theological degree? No. Extensive missionary training? No. A large missions budget? No. A colorful, attention-getting brochure that promised "HOW TO BE SAVED?" No.

What made Matthew such an effective witness was his personal gratitude for what Jesus had done for him. And what was true of Matthew is true of us. Your call to discipleship is from God, of grace, for change, and to share.

THE COMFORTER

John 16:5-11

Jesus spoke the words of John 16:5-11 on Thursday of Passion Week, only hours before His arrest and crucifixion. Even in His last hours, the Savior's first thoughts were for His disciples. And so in a discourse that began in the upper room and continued on the way to Gethsemane—the longest discourse of Jesus recorded in the New Testament and covering John chapters thirteen through seventeen— Jesus sought to prepare His disciples for the troublesome events to come.

"Because I have told you these things," said Jesus, "you are filled with grief." What had He told His disciples that Thursday night? He'd told them that Judas Iscariot would betray Him; that Simon Peter would deny Him; and that all the disciples would be severely persecuted for His name's sake.

And what may have troubled the disciples most were the Savior's references to returning to the Father and their inability to follow. We can easily imagine how the disciples must have felt that evening: Devastated, helpless, hopeless; as if their world were falling to pieces. Surely, all of us have felt the same—not in an upper room or on the road to Gethsemane, but perhaps in our homes, relationships, careers, and finances.

What Jesus told the disciples that Thursday night was not only meant to prepare them for the trouble to come, but to strengthen, encourage, and comfort them. Some of the most familiar and cherished verses of the Bible come from this last great discourse of Jesus. "Do not let your hearts be troubled. Trust in God; trust also in Me," John 14:1. "I am the way and the truth and the life," John 14:6. "Peace I leave with you; My peace I give you," John 14:27. "I am the vine; you are the branches," John 15:5. "Now is your time of grief, but I will see you again and you will rejoice, and no one will take away your joy," John 16:22. Do you recognize these passages? Of course. Do you believe these passages? Yes. Do they bring you comfort? Absolutely. Why? Because of the work of the Holy Spirit.

Six times within John chapters thirteen through seventeen Jesus comforted His troubled disciples with the promise of the Holy Spirit. In four of these instances Jesus referred to the Holy Spirit by the Greek term PARA-CLETOS, transliterated into English as *paraclete*. This Greek word literally means "to call to one's side for the purpose of comforting and encouraging."

Think of the mother who sweeps her crying child into her arms and says, "It's all right. I'm here. I love you. Everything is going to be fine." This is the meaning of the word *paraclete*. And it is also the special work of the Comforter, the Holy Spirit, who comforts us in all our troubles and sorrows by reassuring us with the saving gospel of Jesus Christ.

Jesus told His disciples, "It is for your good that I am going away. Unless I go away, the Counselor will not come to you; but if I go, I will send Him to you," John 16:7. Not seeing Jesus with our eyes may seem anything but "for our good." We often think, "Jesus, if I could only see You with my eyes, I wouldn't worry so much. I wouldn't feel so lonely, depressed, or defeated."

Yet, while we no longer see Jesus with the eyes in our heads, we do see Him with the eyes of our hearts. And through the work of the Holy Spirit, we are closer than ever to Jesus. Not only does He walk beside us, He lives within us. He Himself said, "On that day you will realize that I am in the Father, and you are in Me, and I am in you," John 16:21. How close is that? No matter what troubles you may be facing, remember that the Holy Spirit, the Comforter, is even now calling you to His side to comfort and encourage you with the words of Jesus.

Today, you can buy all sorts of books: Some with eye-catching covers; others with illustrations, cut-outs, and even compact disks. But there is only one book that comes equipped with the Holy Spirit. It's the Bible. Read it. Believe it. And through the Holy Spirit's power be comforted.

THE COST OF DISCIPLESHIP

Luke 14:25-35

As Jesus went about His messianic work, teaching and healing and performing great miracles, large crowds regularly followed Him. And He welcomed them all. But Jesus also wanted the crowds to know about the commitment required to follow Him.

And He spoke of this commitment or "cost" in very stark terms, saying, "If anyone comes to Me and does not hate his father and mother, his wife and children, his brothers and sisters—yes, even his own life—he cannot be My disciple. And anyone who does not carry his cross and follow Me cannot be My disciple." The Savior's intent with these words was not to dissuade people from following Him, but rather to prepare them for the rigors of the journey.

But was Jesus telling us that we must literally hate our parents, siblings, spouses, children, and life itself if we want to be His disciples? No. Such a command would be contrary to other parts of Scripture. For example, in His Sermon on the Mount Jesus warned His disciples against displaying even casual anger, saying, "Anyone who is angry with his brother will be subject to judgment," Matthew 5:22. If Jesus called casual anger wrong, how much more deliberate hatred?

The language Jesus used in Luke 14:26-27 is often called *the language of extreme comparison*. We use this type of comparative language ourselves. "Hey, did you see how fast that car was going? It made our car look like it was going backwards." The meaning of Christ's words was this: Our love for Jesus must be great enough to make all other forms of love appear to be "hatred" by comparison. He must be our first love, first choice, and first priority.

Without this type of committed love, it won't be possible for us to be His disciples. Why? Because following the word, will, and way of Jesus will inevitably bring us into conflict with the word, will, and way of others; perhaps even members of our own family.

Jesus warned His disciples in Matthew 10: "Do not suppose that I have come to bring peace to the earth. I did not come to bring peace, but a sword. For I have come to turn 'a man against his father, a daughter against her mother, a daughter-in-law against her mother-in-law. A man's enemies will be the members of his own household.' Anyone who loves his father or mother more than Me is not worthy of Me."

Yet, when Jesus speaks of the potential costs of discipleship, He also expects that we—people whom He has called by the gospel; people who by grace have come to know Jesus as our Lord and Savior; people whose hearts and minds have been opened by the Spirit of God "to grasp how wide and long and high and deep is the love of Christ, and to know this love that surpasses knowledge," Ephesians

3:18-19—that we will respond, "Oh, yes, Lord! Yes, we will follow You! Because the cost You paid to redeem us makes anything we may suffer or lose for Your sake dim by comparison."

Sadly, not all disciples of Jesus continued to follow Him. We read in John 6: "From this time many of His disciples turned back and no longer followed Him. 'You do not want to leave too, do you?' Jesus asked the Twelve. Simon Peter answered Him, 'Lord, to whom shall we go? You have the words of eternal life. We believe and know that You are the Holy One of God.'"

With this same confession, may each of us gratefully and unswervingly follow the Savior, saying with the hymnist: "Jesus, lead Thou on till our rest is won. And although the way be cheerless, we will follow calm and fearless. Guide us by Thy hand to our fatherland."

THE GOOD PHYSICIAN

Mark 1:29-39

While Jesus did not call Himself "the Good Physician," He came close when He said, "It is not the healthy who need a doctor but the sick. I have not come to call the righteous but sinners to repentance."

The Good Physician Makes House Calls

Today doctors rarely make house calls. Instead, patients make office visits. And this is understandable. Many doctors have large practices. Advanced medical technologies no longer fit easily into black leather satchels. And yet, the modern office visit will never replace the personal touch of the old-fashioned house call—the doctor who came to the home, diagnosed an illness, prescribed a cure, and then stayed for dinner.

Did Jesus, the Good Physician, make house calls? Indeed He did. According to our text, Jesus went "to the home of Simon and Andrew" and healed Simon's mother-in-law of a fever.

But this was not the only house call the Good Physician made. He went to the home of Zacchaeus the tax collector; the home of Simon the Pharisee; the home of Mary, Martha, and Lazarus; the home of the two newlyweds in Cana and the home of the two disciples from Emmaus; the home of

Jairus the synagogue ruler, whose daughter Jesus raised from the dead. (What a house call that was!)

Yes, Jesus healed the multitudes—constantly allowing "office visits" and accepting new patients without proof of medical coverage or demanding copayments. As stated in Mark 1:32-34, "after sunset the people brought to Jesus all the sick and demon-possessed. The whole town gathered at the door, and Jesus healed many who had various diseases."

In these multitudinous healings we see the power of God and His love for the whole world. But in the house calls of Jesus, we also see God's great love for the individual. Amazing, isn't it, that Jesus Christ, the very Son of God, would make one house call to heal one woman of one fever, when many so-called faith-healers today require a TV camera, stage, and packed auditorium.

When you and I face difficulties, we often conclude that God isn't interested or involved. How wrong we are! Our God makes house calls. And He still makes house calls, which means that Jesus is with you in your troubles. Jesus is with you when you roam the lonely halls of an empty house. Jesus is with you when you lose a loved one. Jesus is with you in your sicknesses, marriage, financial troubles, and doubts. Jesus is with you on the operating table and with you especially when you think He is not. He knows your house address—and has for all eternity.

The Good Physician Heals

Does the Good Physician still heal sicknesses today? Absolutely. Where does the Bible say that He stopped? I tend to agree with Benjamin Franklin, who said, "God heals and the doctors take the fee." Does this mean that God will heal every sickness? No. In His infinite knowledge and care, the Good Physician may allow an illness as a 'cure' to strengthen faith. Paul spoke of having a 'thorn in the flesh'—perhaps a frustrating, painful medical condition. Three times he asked God to remove this thorn. God's answer? "My grace is sufficient for you, for My power is made perfect in weakness," 2 Corinthians 12:9.

Yet, the healing the Good Physician brings far transcends bodily healing to embrace healing of the mind, heart, and spirit. "By His wounds we are healed," wrote the prophet Isaiah. And what a remarkable passage this is—the knowledge that the bloody wounds which resulted in the Savior's death were at the same time the very wounds that brought us life, hope, forgiveness, and eternal salvation.

Wounds which heal the disease of sin. Wounds which heal broken homes and marriages. Wounds which heal the pain of regret. Wounds which, through the power of the gospel, heal our very lives; and at the touch of the Good Physician, empower us to rise from our beds of hopelessness and despair and get on with life—the way Simon's mother-in-law rose from her bed and began to joyfully serve Jesus.

THE GREAT TRUTHS OF CHRISTMAS

John 1:1-14

For weeks we anticipate Christmas and relish each sign of its coming: lights and decorations, Christmas trees and Christmas cards; mistletoe, fruitcake, and gift-giving. And then Christmas is over. Each day beyond Christmas, it is more difficult to maintain a yuletide spirit. By the end of January, the most festive among us are wondering, "When will the neighbors get that manger scene off the front lawn?"

It is possible to have the same reaction with the Christmas message. After four weeks of Advent, Christmas Eve, Christmas Day, the Sunday after Christmas, and the first Sunday in Epiphany—one of the readings is traditionally the visit of the Magi—we may start to wonder, "When will the church calendar get the manger and Magi off the front lawn?"

Yet, as John 1:1-14 reminds us, the great truths of Christmas are not seasonal but eternal, and meant to give us joy and hope every day of the year. While there are many truths of Christmas, perhaps the greatest truths involve the Person of Christ.

Jesus Christ is True God
There are many Bible passages that attest to the deity of Christ. One of these is John 1:1. "In the beginning was the Word, and the Word was with God, and the Word was

God." The baby Jesus born in Bethlehem and wrapped in swaddling clothes was and is truly and fully God. The 12-year-old Jesus in the temple who taught and astonished the Jewish doctors of theology; the historical Jesus who walked the shores of Lake Galilee, leaving sandal-prints in the sand; the Jesus who died on Good Friday and was raised triumphantly on Easter Sunday—was and is truly and fully God.

As the Christmas prophecy declared, "The virgin will be with child and will give birth to a Son, and they will call Him Immanuel—which means, 'God with us,' " Matthew 1:23. GOD with us. And if God is with us, is there anything in our lives—financial troubles, difficult relationships, job loss, aches and pains, and even death itself—that can be against us and overcome us? No. This reality brings Christmas joy throughout the year, doesn't it?

Jesus Christ is True Man

God has all power to solve all problems, but does He have the willingness? This question is answered by the second great truth of Christmas; namely, God's willingness to humble Himself to death, to become truly human, in order to save us from our sins.

Everything wrong with our world is the result of Adam and Eve in pride aspiring to become God. Everything right with our lives—forgiveness, salvation, peace and joy—is the result of God in humility aspiring to become man. If God was willing to become human for us, will He not always be willing to help us in every other way? Of course. The cross proves His willingness.

More than this, in becoming true man Jesus also experienced all of our human problems; yet remained without sin. You and I can never rightly say, "God, You don't understand what I'm going through." God went through it.

This is why Scripture says, "We do not have a high priest who is unable to sympathize with our weaknesses, but we have one who has been tempted in every way, just as we are—yet was without sin. Let us then approach the throne of grace with confidence, so that we may receive mercy and find grace to help us in our time of need," Hebrews 4:15-16.

Jesus is true God. Jesus is true man. Don't just recite these great truths of Christmas; live them. Let every day be a Christmas Day.

WISDOM AND FOLLY

Proverbs 9

"I shall be telling this with a sigh somewhere ages and ages hence: Two roads diverged in a yellow wood, and I—I took the road less traveled by, and that has made all the difference." The words are from Robert Frost's poem *The Road Not Taken*. In it Frost describes two roads diverging in a yellow wood and the necessity of choosing one road over the other.

Life is like that poem. You and I face choices on a daily basis. Some are minor, but others are very important: "Should I tell a convenient lie or speak the painful truth? Should I teach my children to love money or to love God? Should I live my own way or live God's way?" Solomon addressed these questions in Proverbs 9. He did not use the illustration of two diverging roads, but the invitations of two different women: One named Wisdom and the other named Folly.

In Frost's poem the diverging roads looked similar. "Just as fair," he wrote. In Proverbs 9 Folly attempts to look like Wisdom. She locates herself at the same place: "the highest point of the city," verses 3 and 14. She addresses the same audience and extends the same word-for-word invitation: "Let all who are simple come in here," verses 4 and 16.

Even today the unsuspecting confuse Wisdom and Folly. "The Bible or the Koran; what's the difference? Jesus or Buddha; what's the difference? Creation or evolution; what's the difference? Grace or works; what's the difference?"

However, the Biblical definition of wisdom is unmistakably clear and has nothing to do with intelligence quotients or report cards or academic degrees. Solomon wrote, "The fear of the LORD is the beginning of wisdom, and the knowledge of the Holy One is understanding," Proverbs 9:10. To fear the LORD is to have a holy reverence for the LORD; the knowledge of who God is and what God is like and what God has done for us through Jesus Christ—the knowledge that God loves the sinner but hates sin.

Scripture insists that true wisdom comes from God, and that the truly wise person believes in Jesus Christ as Lord and Savior. As Paul wrote to Timothy, "From infancy you have known the holy Scriptures, which are able to make you wise for salvation through faith in Christ Jesus," 2 Timothy 3:15. This does not mean that earthly wisdom has no value. Go to school. Get a good education. Learn reading, writing, and arithmetic. Continue to do the New York Times crossword puzzle and blurt out answers to *Jeopardy* and *Wheel of Fortune*.

However, never forget that mathematics cannot teach you how to be saved or how to lead a God-pleasing life. Never forget that geometry cannot bring you to Christ, of whom the apostle Paul wrote, "In Christ are hidden all the treasures of wisdom and knowledge," Colossians 2:3. And

189

never forget that God's wisdom is diametrically opposed to human wisdom—that giving is better than receiving; that humility leads to greatness; that Jesus Christ redeemed the world through His suffering, death, and resurrection. All foolishness to the world. All wisdom to God.

Jesus did not write a poem about two roads diverging in a yellow wood; however, He did speak about two diverging roads—and which one to choose: "Enter through the narrow gate. For wide is the gate and broad is the road that leads to destruction, and many enter through it. But small is the gate and narrow the road that leads to life, and only a few find it," Matthew 7:13-14.

THE JOURNEY TO CHRIST

Matthew 2:1-12

The story of the wise men is the story of individuals who were led to Christ from afar. As such, their journey is our journey, and the journey of everyone led by the Holy Spirit to recognize Jesus as Lord and Savior.

A Journey of God's Faithfulness

The wise men journeyed to Israel to see "the one who has been born king of the Jews," Matthew 2:2. But what if Jesus had not been born? What if God had changed His mind? There would be no Christ, no Christmas, no salvation, no journey of the wise men to Christ, and no journey to Christ of our own.

But God kept His promise to send Jesus. In fact, the coming of Jesus fulfilled more than three hundred Old Testament prophecies; not one forgotten, discarded, or broken. The coming of Jesus is also God's guarantee that He will keep all His other promises to us—the promise to never leave us, always love us, deliver us from trouble, and bring us safely through this life to the next. Paul wrote in 2 Corinthians 1:20, "For no matter how many promises God has made, they are 'Yes' in Christ."

A Journey of God's Grace

Grace means God's undeserved favor in Christ; that God does the doing and we do the receiving. And so it was with the journey of the wise men. God provided the Savior. God created the miraculous star. God enabled the wise men to recognize this star as Christ's star—"We saw *His* star in the east," Matthew 2:2. God led the wise men to Christ and led them to believe in Christ. And in leading the wise men to Christ, God demonstrated His grace in another way; namely, by presenting Jesus as the Savior of all people, both Jews and Gentiles. The wise men were Gentiles.

Our journey to Christ is no less a miracle of God's grace. It doesn't matter who we are, where we live, what we own; whether we are young or old, rich or poor, black or white; whether we ride a camel or drive a Ford. Jesus Christ is the Savior of all. There are no differences between human beings where differences count, as Paul wrote in Romans 3:22-23, "There is no difference, for all have sinned and fall short of the glory of God, and are justified freely by His grace through the redemption that came by Christ Jesus."

A Journey of Faith Created by God's Word

The wise men did not find Christ on their own. They followed God's star and God's word. And what did they find when they arrived in Bethlehem? Not a palace, but a simple house in a sleepy, little town. Not luxuries, but bare necessities. Not throngs of servants, but Jesus with His mother. Not a crown, but a crude cradle. Not a display of kingly power, but a display of utmost humility—a little child, who at this time was likely less than two years old.

But did the wise men look at each other with incredulousness? Did they recheck the position of the star and the address of the house? No, they believed. They "bowed down and worshiped Him," Matthew 2:11. Through God's guiding word, the wise men were given the faith to recognize the son of Mary as the Son of God.

God leads us to Christ in the same way, namely, through His word. This is why hearing and reading the word of God are so important. Paul wrote in 2 Timothy 3:15, "From infancy you have known the holy scriptures, which are able to make you *wise* for salvation through faith in Christ Jesus."

Following God's word is what made the wise men wise. It's what makes us wise men and wise women too.

THE KING AND I

Revelation 1:4-8

We live in a time of great fear. A time of increasing chaos, conflict, and calamity. A time in which terrorist groups are attempting to outdo each other in carnage and death. A time in which right is wrong, evil abounds, and occultism and witchcraft are openly practiced. A time in which Christianity is under fierce attack.

"There will be terrible times in the last days," Paul wrote in 2 Timothy 3:1. And we are witnessing the fulfillment of this prophecy daily on FOX News, CNN, and MSNBC. In such terrible times, you and I need to be reminded that JESUS CHRIST IS KING; that JESUS CHRIST IS CONTROLLING ALL THINGS—the universe, the Christian Church, and every detail of our individual lives. This is the constant refrain of Revelation. And it is the special message of Revelation 1:4-8.

Jesus, the Supreme King

Not a day passes when we fail to hear the plans of earthly rulers. 'The President plans to do this. The Prime Minister plans to do that. ISIS threatens this. North Korea threatens that.' Yet, despite what we read in the daily newspaper or hear on the nightly news, presidents, prime ministers, ISIS, and North Korea are not controlling world events. Jesus Christ our King is. He is "the ruler of the kings of the earth," Revelation 1:5. Throughout history God has moved kings and kingdoms to serve His divine purposes. And the same is true today.

Even the crucifixion of Christ happened—not because the Jewish religious leaders plotted it, or the mob demanded it, or Pilate allowed it, but because God ordained it from eternity to save lost humanity. "Indeed Herod and Pontius Pilate met together with the Gentiles and the people of Israel in this city to conspire against Your holy servant Jesus, whom You anointed. They did what Your power and will had decided beforehand should happen," Acts 4:27-28. When frightened by the world or personal events, remind yourself: "Jesus Christ is in complete control. I'm not alone. It's *the King and I.*

Jesus, the Faithful King

In Revelation 1:5 Jesus is called "the faithful witness." The Greek is more literally, 'the witness, the faithful one,' with the emphasis on faithful. Can you name one president, prime minister, dictator, congressman, or career politician to whom the word FAITHFUL can be constantly applied— faithful to duty, faithful to office, faithful to campaign promises, or faithful to constituents? No.

Jesus Christ is such a faithful King. Faithful to His word. Faithful to His calling. Faithful to His promises. Faithful to the point of death. In Scripture the faithfulness of Christ is viewed as the absolute proof that God will keep all His promises to us. As Paul wrote in 2 Corinthians 1: "For no matter how many promises God has made, they are 'Yes' in Christ."

If you are wondering, "Will God keep all of His promises to me—His promise to protect, provide, forgive, strengthen, save, and deliver me safely from this life to the next?" The answer is, YES. Remind yourself: *The King and I.* Others may fail you, but this King will not.

Jesus, the Loving King

Some Bible verses seem to encapsulate the whole gospel message. Revelation 1:5 is one of them: "To Him who loves us and has freed us from our sins by His blood." In Greek the verb "freed us" is in the Aorist tense, which is a tense of completed action. When Jesus Christ died on the cross, He made complete atonement for our sins. Nothing was left undone. We were set free and washed clean through the once-for-all sacrifice of Christ. "The blood of Jesus Christ, His Son, purifies us from *all* sin," 1 John 1:7.

The other verb in Revelation 1:5, "loves us," is in the present tense; that is, the tense of ongoing, uninterrupted action. In other words, the love of our gracious King, Jesus Christ, is always present, even when we think it is not. He is loving us in the good times. He is still loving us through the bad times. And it is this immeasurable, unstoppable love of the King that determines every aspect of the way He governs our lives.

If tempted to doubt God's love for you, remember: *The King and I.* Remember what the King sacrificed to save you. Remember that His love moved Him to make that sacrifice, and that His sacrifice is the undeniable proof of His love.

Jesus, the Coming King

"Look," commands Revelation 1:7, "He is coming with the clouds, and every eye will see Him, even those who pierced Him; and all the peoples of the earth will mourn because of Him. So shall it be. Amen." Do you sense any uncertainty in this verse about the return of Christ? No. Instead we are told: He is coming. Every eye will see Him. People will mourn because of Him. And then the solemn declaration of truth, "So shall it be. Amen."

When the King does return, you and I will finally see Him as He is, and realize the consummation of all our hopes—that described so beautifully in Revelation 7: "Therefore, they are before the throne of God and serve Him day and night in His temple; and He who sits on the throne will spread His tent over them. Never again will they hunger; never again will they thirst. The sun will not beat upon them, nor any scorching heat. For the Lamb at the center of the throne will be their shepherd; He will lead them to springs of living water. And God will wipe away every tear from their eyes."

When life seems too hard and burdens too heavy, remember that your King is coming again—and soon. And when He returns, you will be able to say for all eternity: *The King and I.*

Jesus, the Complete King

In Revelation 1:8 Jesus says of Himself: " 'I am the Alpha and the Omega,' says the Lord God, 'who is, and who was, and who is to come, the Almighty.' " Alpha and

197

Omega are the beginning and end, the first and last letters, of the Greek alphabet, equivalent to our A and Z. And when applied to Jesus, the name "Alpha and Omega" has wondrous meaning. He is the eternal King, "who is, and who was, and who is to come." He is the Creator-King, the Source (Alpha) and Consummation (Omega) of all things. And He is the All-Sufficient King.

Perhaps you've heard advertisements from retailers who promise: "We stock everything you need from A to Z." The same idea is contained in the beautiful name "Alpha and Omega." Jesus Christ, our great God and King, is everything we need in life from A to Z. As expressed in one hymn: "Just as I am, poor, wretched, blind; sight, riches, healing of the mind; yes, *all I need in Thee to find*, O Lamb of God, I come. I come."

In Revelation 4 the apostle John is invited to step through an 'open door' in heaven in order to see the behind-the-scenes reality of GOD IN CONTROL; to see the ultimate end of evil and the ultimate victory of the Christian Church and each Christian individual. But before he is permitted to step through that door, he is first given the beautiful vision of Jesus Christ in Revelation 1—Jesus, the KING OF KINGS and the LORD OF LORDS; "the ruler of the kings of the earth."

Before you and I walk through any door in our lives, let us have the same view of our eternal, omnipotent King. Let's walk through those doors saying, "The King and I."

THE LORD IS MY SHEPHERD

Psalm 23

Before David was the king of Israel, he was a shepherd who tended the flocks of his father Jesse; and as such he clearly understood the importance of leading sheep to green pastures, protecting them from enemies, and bringing them safely home.

Yet, as meaningful as these activities were to David as a shepherd, they were even more meaningful to David as one of the "sheep;" a man who had been shepherded by the LORD through every step and stage of life: beginnings and endings, peaks and valleys, ups and downs.

Psalm 23, however, isn't just about David's life; it is also about the way in which the LORD leads us through life. David wrote the words, but we can claim the pronouns: "*My* shepherd. *I* shall not want. He leadeth *me*. He restoreth *my* soul. Though *I* walk through the valley. *I* will dwell in the house of the LORD forever."

It's the personal nature of Psalm 23 that leads us to cherish it so—a personal psalm, personalized message, and most of all, a God who personally shepherds us through life. Indeed, of all the images of Jesus in Christian art, what image is more endearing than that of the Good Shepherd bringing one lost lamb home to God, safe in His arms and next to His heart?

Centuries before the birth of Jesus the prophet Isaiah wrote of Him: "He tends His flock like a shepherd. He gathers the lambs in His arms and carries them close to His heart," Isaiah 40:11.

The beautiful images in Psalm 23 reflect the many blessings ours in Jesus Christ—rest, restoration, safety, endurance, salvation, and eternal life. However, the first verse of this psalm is without question the most important verse, because every other verse and blessing in the psalm flow from its promise.

Only when the LORD is our shepherd can we truly say, "I shall not want." Only when the LORD leads are "goodness and mercy" sure to follow. Everything depends upon following the right shepherd; and that right Shepherd is Jesus Christ.

Scripture contains many names for God, and each name describes some aspect of His divine nature. The name for God in Psalm 23:1 is YAVEH in Hebrew, or as it came to be pronounced, "Jehovah."

Jehovah is actually a Hebrew verb that means "I AM." This is the one name of God perhaps more than any other that describes the lasting nature of His love, grace, mercy, and promises. He is the only Shepherd who will never forsake us. He is the only Shepherd who will always lead us safely to green pastures and quiet waters, through peaks and valleys, until we dwell in His house forever.

I can think of no more fitting summary of Psalm 23 than the precious hymn verse many of us learned as children: "I am Jesus' little lamb. Ever glad at heart I am. For my Shepherd gently guides me. Knows my need and well provides me. Loves me every day the same. Even calls me by my name."

Though we teach these words to children, don't think of them as childish. To say "I am Jesus' little lamb" is the essence of a *childlike* faith.

THE MESSAGE OF THE CROSS

1 Corinthians 1:18

Many years ago I enrolled in a university history course. The first few classes were enjoyable. But one day, the subject of Jesus came up. How or why I no longer remember. What I do remember is the way in which a young man snorted at the mere mention of the Lord's name and declared, "Jesus was a homosexual. Why else would He have never married? Why were all His first disciples men?"

I was stunned. Yes, I knew that hatred of the Lord Jesus existed; but I had never heard it expressed with such vitriolic contempt. The classroom erupted into knee-slapping laughter. Eventually, even the professor joined in.

But then I'm certain the guards who blindfolded, beat, and spit upon Jesus laughed at Him in the same derisive way. "The men who were guarding Jesus began mocking and beating Him. They blindfolded Him and demanded, 'Prophesy! Who hit You?' And they said many other insulting things to Him," Luke 22:63-65. From ancient courtrooms to modern classrooms, ridicule of Jesus and His cross has continued unabated. Why?

The World Calls the Cross "Foolish"
Paul provides the answer in 1 Corinthians 1:18, saying, "For the message of the cross is foolishness to those who are

perishing." The Greek word translated as "foolishness" in this verse, MORIA, is related to our English word MORONIC.

Worldly wisdom finds everything about Jesus and God's plan of salvation moronic and foolish. How could a Savior of any significance be born in a barn; or live in poverty; or have no place to call home; or choose simple fishermen as disciples; or associate with the dregs and outcasts of society; or ride triumphantly into Jerusalem on a lowly donkey? Nonsense. A knee-slapping joke to the world, whose idea of success is always based on power, wealth, charisma, and having the right connections.

Despite the multitude of Old Testament prophecies about the Messiah—details as incredibly specific as "He was despised and rejected by men, a man of sorrows, and familiar with suffering," Isaiah 53:3—the majority of Jews rejected Jesus as the long-awaited Savior because He did not meet their messianic expectations.

The citizens of His own hometown, Nazareth, "took offense at Him," Matthew 13:57. Literally, they were 'scandalized' by Jesus. And what finally could be more scandalous than the notion of a Savior who won eternal salvation by suffering and dying on a cross?

Equally scandalous to worldly wisdom is that Christians should believe in such a Savior; more than this, that we should want to remember the Savior's passion, whether by celebrating the Lord's Supper or special Lenten services. Yet, ironically, what the world calls wisdom, God calls foolishness. What the world calls really living, God calls really perishing.

Sadly, when people scoff at the cross and reject Jesus, it isn't because of any academic superiority—as was the belief of that young man who scorned Jesus in history class; it is because they are perishing. Paul wrote in 2 Corinthians 4: "And even if our gospel is veiled, it is veiled to those who are perishing. The god of this age has blinded the minds of unbelievers, so that they cannot see the light of the gospel of the glory of Christ, who is the image of God."

God Calls the Cross "Power"
Once the familiar "T" shape of the cross brought only terror. Crucifixion was designed to be excruciatingly painful. In fact, the term *excruciating* is derived from the Latin *excruciatus*, which literally means "out of the cross."

The agony lasted for hours, at times even days. The physical torture was unspeakable. Nails were driven through the wrists and feet. It was impossible to support the weight of the body. Shoulders, elbows, and wrists became dislocated.

The position of the victim on the cross also made it virtually impossible to breathe, particularly to exhale. The only way to exhale was to pull oneself up on the cross, putting weight on the nails in both hands and feet. Death was often related to suffocation. And along with the physical torture of crucifixion came such psychological torture as the constant gasping for breath and the shame of being crucified naked.

Truly, we have no conception of what our Savior suffered for us on the cross. His physical suffering was gruesome in itself. But at the same time, He was also carrying the weight of the world's sin and experiencing the agonies of hell—and all of this for *our* sakes.

Isaiah wrote: "Surely He took up our infirmities and carried our sorrows, yet we considered Him stricken by God, smitten by Him, and afflicted. But He was pierced for our transgressions, He was crushed for our iniquities; the punishment that brought us peace was upon Him, and by His wounds we are healed. We all, like sheep, have gone astray, each of us has turned to his own way; and the LORD laid on Him the iniquity of us all," Isaiah 53:4-6.

For believers, however, the familiar "T" shape of the cross has become a symbol of triumph and transformation; a symbol we humbly display in our churches and homes, and wear as necklaces and pendants. For by God's grace and Spirit, we've come to see the message of the cross as a message of power, hope, and salvation—not defeat, but everlasting triumph; not weakness, but God's omnipotent strength; not failure, but God's unlimited forgiveness.

The message of the cross has the power not only to save us but to transform us; that is, to empower us to live grateful lives befitting so great a salvation. Paul wrote of this transformation in Galatians 2:20, saying: "I have been crucified with Christ and I"—significantly, the Greek word for "I" is *EGO*—"no longer live, but Christ lives in me. The life I live in the body, I live by faith in the Son of God, who loved me and gave Himself for me."

Can we truly stand before the cross of Jesus, see Him suffer so much for our sakes, and yet walk away unmoved? Can we see what He paid for our forgiveness, and yet refuse to forgive others? Can we understand how His death reconciled the world to God, and yet still insist we have irreconcilable differences? No.

THE ONE THING NEEDED

Luke 10:38-42

Martha was not a bad person. Martha was a distracted person, distracted from the word of God by all the dinner "preparations that had to be made," Luke 10:40. Her intentions were right. Her priorities were wrong. And so Jesus told her, "Martha, Martha, you are worried and upset by many things, but only one thing is needed," Luke 10:41-42.

Like Martha, we too have many responsibilities. Going to work. Earning a living. Caring for families. Eating right. Exercising regularly. Rotating the tires. Changing the oil. Walking the dog. These are wholesome activities, though some are more pressing than others.

Yet, the question raised by Christ's words to Martha—"only one thing is needed"—is simply this: Are any of our responsibilities, activities, or commitments more important than hearing the word of God? According to Jesus, the answer is NO. Why is God's word so essential to our lives?

God Blesses Us through His Word

Jesus said plainly in Luke 11:28, "Blessed are they who hear the word of God and keep it." In Scripture blessedness also has the sense of happiness and completeness. Do you want happiness? Do you want to feel complete? Where you should turn? Of course, to the "one thing needed."

Unfortunately, at times we view church-going as doing something nice for God. "Here I am God. I got up early, put on my best clothes, drove many miles. You can thank me later." This is wrong. When we go to church, we're not doing something nice for God; He is doing something powerful and miraculous to us, namely, blessing us through His word.

Through His Word God Gives Us Everything We Need for Time and Eternity

He creates faith. He bestows salvation. He provides wisdom and shows us how to live. He teaches us absolute truth instead of the moral relativism of our world. In other words, through the Bible God equips us for every situation, every condition, and every problem in life.

Paul wrote to Timothy, "All Scripture is given by inspiration of God, and is profitable for doctrine, for reproof, for correction, for instruction in righteousness, that the man of God may be complete, thoroughly equipped for every good work," 2 Timothy 3:16-17.

Through His Word God Reveals the One Way to be Saved; namely, through Faith in Jesus Christ

You won't find this truth in any other so-called sacred writing. Only the Bible teaches that "a man is not justified by observing the law, but by faith in Jesus Christ," Galatians

2:15-16. So how important should the Bible be to us? How much do we need it?

Yes, at times the Bible appears small and ordinary compared to the enormity of our problems. When in trouble, we wonder how it can help us. When visiting hospital rooms and funeral homes, we wonder how it can comfort us.

But have we forgotten? "By the word of the LORD were the heavens made," Psalm 33:6. By the word of the LORD, aged Abraham and barren Sarah became the parents of nations. By the word of the LORD, Jesus raised dead-and-buried Lazarus from his grave.

In the end, making God's word the top priority in our lives is a choice. As Jesus told Martha, "Mary has chosen what is better, and it will not be taken away from her."

What choice will we make?

THE ONE WAY

John 14:1-12

In a single verse composed of two simple sentences, Jesus declared Himself to be the only way to God the Father and the only way to be saved.

The Comprehensiveness

Jesus said, "I am the way and the truth and the life. No one comes to the Father except through Me," John 14:6. This is a clear, comprehensive, and unmistakable statement. From the "I am" at its beginning to the "through Me" at its end, the emphasis is entirely on Jesus Christ as the only Savior.

Notice the use of the definite article "the" in John 14:6. Jesus is not one way, one truth, and one life among many. He is *the* way and *the* truth and *the* life—meaning there is no other.

Furthermore, Jesus not only has the way, truth, and life. He Himself is the way and the truth and the life. The way, truth, and life are found only in Him. Therefore, anyone who has a personal relationship with Jesus Christ by faith also has the way to God, the truth of God, and the life from God.

The Conflict

Of course, to declare, as Jesus did, that He alone is the world's Savior, is to immediately draw the wrath and scorn of the unbelieving. "You can't say that," they insist. "To say that Jesus alone saves is to be intolerant, arrogant, unloving, and un-American." Sound familiar?

Sadly, some Christian churches today soften or even eliminate these words of Jesus; at least those churches more concerned with statistics and political correctness than ministry and truth. "We can't confess such a thing publicly," they say. "To do so would be to offend the Muslims, Mormons, Jehovah's Witnesses, Scientologists, and many others. These groups are willing to acknowledge Jesus as a good man and a great prophet. Isn't that enough?"

No, it is not enough—not according to Scripture, and not according to the plain words of Jesus in John 14:6. And there are many other Bible passages which present Jesus Christ as the only way to be saved. Among them, John 3:16, "For God so loved the world that He gave His only begotten Son, that whoever believes in Him should not perish but have everlasting life." Or John 17:3, "And this is eternal life, that they may know You, the only true God, and Jesus Christ whom You have sent." Or Acts 4:12, where the apostle Peter says of Jesus, "Nor is there salvation in any other, for there is no other name under heaven given among men by which we must be saved."

The Comfort

"I am the way and the truth and the life." For a believer these words of Jesus bring the utmost comfort. Never forget the context in which Jesus spoke these words—not a seminary class or study group or general pastoral conference.

When Jesus said, "I am the way," He was addressing dearly loved disciples, who had heard Him speak of betrayal, denial, suffering, death, resurrection, and returning to the Father. Understandably, they were worried and afraid.

Fear and worry were the context in which Jesus promised, "I am the way and the truth and the life." At their simplest, these words of the Savior tell us that when we embrace Him by faith, we have everything we need to be saved; everything we need for time and eternity.

No matter what burdens we bring to Jesus, no matter what questions we ask of Jesus, His answer is always the same. "I am the way."

THE RIGHT ATTITUDE

Philippians 2:5-11

Two thousand years ago, the cross of Jesus was firmly planted in the rocky soil of Golgotha. Since that time, it has been planted in countless human hearts through the message of "Christ crucified."

The cross of Jesus, so central to our salvation, is also central to our Christian behavior. This is why the New Testament presents Jesus as the Model and Motivation for Christian living. It encourages us to love as Jesus loved, serve as Jesus served, and forgive as Jesus forgave. In Philippians 2:5-11, the apostle Paul exhorts us to have the same attitude Jesus had.

But what type of attitude did Jesus have? An attitude of humility. An attitude that did not insist on personal rights, but rather served others and spared no cost in doing what needed to be done.

Though Jesus was true God, He "did not consider equality with God something to be grasped," that is, something to be held onto at all costs, "but made Himself nothing, taking the very nature of a servant." Outside of Mark Twain's fictional story of *The Prince and the Pauper*, how many factual princes, presidents, or kings have willingly laid aside their wealth, power, and prestige in order to serve others? Yet, Jesus did, and Jesus is God.

Jesus Christ—born in a barn, not a palace. He was poor, not rich. He had no place to call home or lay His head. He rode triumphantly into Jerusalem on a lowly beast of burden, not on a prancing white war stallion. Finally, He was nailed to a cross.

From incarnation to crucifixion, Jesus humbled Himself in order to redeem us from our sins. Imagine how His type of humble, selfless attitude will empower our lives, marriages, ministries, and relationships.

THE RIGHT CONNECTION

John 15:1-8

Having the right connection is important in life. This is true at many levels, including cell phone calls, appliances, relationships, job searches, travel arrangements, and even linking a perpetrator to a crime.

John 15:1-8 is also about having the right connection. Using the simple but vivid analogy of a vine and its branches, Jesus taught the crucial importance of being connected to Him by faith. Yet, we don't need a vineyard to understand the lessons of the vine and branches. The same lessons are taught by virtually every plant, shrub, and weed. What are the lessons?

The Right Vine

The right connection starts with the right vine. Jesus said, "I am the true vine,' John 15:1. The original Greek is more emphatic, literally, 'I am the vine, the true one.' True. Genuine. Real. Authentic.

How many Bible passages can you recite that proclaim Jesus to be the one true way to salvation? Jesus Himself declared, "I am the way and the truth and the life. No one comes to the Father except through Me," John 14:6. Simon Peter insisted, "Nor is there salvation in any other, for there is no other name under heaven given among men by which we must be saved." Acts 4:12. John wrote in his First

Epistle, "The blood of Jesus, His Son, purifies us from all sin," 1 John 1:7. What these and many other Bible passages teach verbally, Jesus taught visually with the example of the vine and its branches.

Sadly, there are as many religious counterfeits and fake messiahs as there are plastic plants. History is littered with them—names like Buddha, Krishna, Jim Jones, Modern Science, Advanced Technology, and Money In The Bank. "Believe in us," they all say, "and you will be saved."

But there is only one true vine and one true Savior, Jesus Christ. And this reality is as comforting as it is sobering. It tells me that no matter who I am, what I've done, what I own, or where I live, as long as I am connected to Jesus through faith, I am saved. Through that connection I obtain forgiveness and salvation, and share in Christ's indestructible life and overwhelming victory.

A Lasting Connection
The right connection is also a lasting connection. Every Christian should know what every gardener knows; namely, that a branch exists only because of the vine. A branch does not grow the vine; the vine grows the branch. If all blessings come to us through Christ, do we need to be told to stay connected to Christ? Jesus thought so. He used the word "remain" eight times in John 15:1-8.

The temptation to believe that we no longer need Jesus, or that we no longer need the support, strength, and stability of the vine, comes in many forms. Yet, if we think we can do anything without Jesus Christ—whether securing eternal salvation or daily bread; solving problems at home or problems at the office; tossing restlessly in our bed or sitting endlessly by the hospital bed of a loved one—we need to hear the Savior's words: "Apart from Me you can do nothing," John 15:5.

Can a branch survive when torn from its vine? No. But then the opposite is also true. If we can do nothing apart from Christ, what can we accomplish through our connection to Christ? Let the apostle Paul answer. He said, "I can do *everything* through Him who gives me strength," Philippians 4:13.

This is where we find the strength to deal with the loss of a loved one; the strength to spend hours caring for a sick parent, spouse, or child; the strength to face financial worries and troubled marriages and heartache and pain and even the end of life itself. Because when we have a lasting connection to Christ the vine, the strength is not ours. The strength is His.

A Clean Connection

Jesus said, "I am the true vine, and my Father is the gardener. He cuts off every branch in Me that does not bear fruit, while every branch that does bear fruit He prunes so that it will be even more fruitful. You are already clean because of the word I have spoken to you," John 15:1-3.

The word "prunes" in verse 2 and "clean" in verse 3 are actually from the same Greek word, KATHARIZO, from which we derive the English term catharsis. When a branch is pruned, it is cleaned. Pruning is essential for a branch's life, beauty, shape, strength, and most of all, its fruitfulness. This is a fact of nature. It is also a fact about faith.

Whether God the Gardener prunes our lives through His word or prunes our lives through difficulties—cleaning out harmful thoughts and wrong directions, an unhealthy reliance on self or material possessions—we should praise Him for His loving care. For by such pruning He teaches us the importance of staying connected to Jesus and makes our faith more and more productive.

The author of Hebrews wrote: "No discipline is pleasant at the time, but painful. Later on, however, it produces a HARVEST of righteousness and peace for those who have been trained by it," Hebrews 12:11.

THE SECRET OF CONTENTMENT

Philippians 4:10-13

Contentment is a Secret

"I have learned the secret of contentment," Paul wrote. But how is biblical contentment a secret? Each year more than 100 million Bibles are sold, and the secret of contentment is contained in each one.

The Greek word Paul used for "secret" is related to our word *mystery*. It is not that God's message of contentment is unknown. It's that by nature human beings do not believe this message. Instead, they pursue other means of contentment, mistakenly believing that contentment can be found on a shelf at Walmart or Macy's; or by inserting a crisp dollar bill into a lottery vending machine.

Contentment is Learned

Paul wrote: "I have learned to be content," 4:11; and again, "I have learned the secret of being content," 4:12. *Learned* is an important word in this context. Contentment cannot be inherited or purchased, it must be learned. And learning is a process. The more we learn from Scripture, the more content we will be.

The apostle Paul himself had to learn contentment. Both the good times and the bad times in his life were his teachers; the "whatever the circumstances," 4:10; the "need or plenty," 4:11; the "well fed or hungry," 4:12.

Through these changing circumstances, Paul learned that his contentment in Jesus Christ was unchanging.

Contentment is not Based on Personal Circumstances

While contentment is learned through circumstances, it can never be based on circumstances. You've likely heard this type of conversation. "How have you been, Tom?" And Tom answers: "I'm great. I graduated from college. I got a job with a starting salary of $60,000 a year. And Marilyn and I are getting married. I'm so happy. I'm so content."

Only, how content would Tom be if he had failed to graduate; or if he lost his new job; or if Marilyn suddenly canceled the wedding? This is why contentment based on situations will always be situational contentment. It can never last. It can never satisfy.

However, the type of contentment Paul wrote about in Philippians 4:10-13 is not based on circumstances, but is independent of them. Listen again to his words: "I have learned to be content whatever the circumstances," 4:11. "I have learned the secret of being content in any and every situation," 4:12.

The Secret of Contentment

What, then, is the secret of contentment? Paul answered this question in Philippians 4:13, providing us with some of the most important, powerful information we will ever know or share with our loved ones and friends. And to think he offered this information in the middle of a four-chapter thank-you note to the Philippians—while chained in a damp, dark, rat-infested prison. He said, "I can do everything through Him who gives me strength." The Greek word translated as strength in this verse is DUNAMIS, from which we derive our English word *dynamite*. Do you truly think that there is any circumstance, any situation, that the power of Jesus Christ cannot enable you to endure or overcome?

Someone once observed—and I'm paraphrasing: 'Placing everything into the right hands is what really matters. In my hands a basketball is worth twenty-dollars. In the hands of LeBron James it is worth millions. In my hands a staff can help me walk. In the hands of Moses it parted the Red Sea. In my hands nails can build a birdhouse. In the hands of Christ they resulted in salvation for the world.'

Place your dreams, desires, goals, relationships, indeed, your entire life into the capable hands of Jesus Christ, and you will find true contentment.

THE TIE THAT BINDS

1 Corinthians 1:10-17

The Apostle Paul arrived in Corinth in 51 or 52 A.D. At that time, Corinth was the capital of Roman Achaia, and may have had a population greater than 750,000—similar to that of San Francisco or Indianapolis. There were shops, inns, and pubs; an amphitheater capable of seating 14,000; a concert hall for musical performances and poetry competitions; a sports stadium for the Isthmian Games; and several magnificent temples dedicated to Hermes, Apollo, Venus, Isis, Demeter, and Asclepius.

Along with rampant idolatry, Corinth was known for its immorality. In fact, the Greek word CORINTHIAZOMAI, literally "to Corinthianize," was synonymous with "to fornicate." Yet, here Paul preached the saving gospel of Jesus Christ. By God's grace, many Corinthians came to believe. When Paul left Corinth after eighteen months, he left behind a growing Christian congregation.

The Trouble Begins

But around 57 or 58 A.D., Paul received word that the Corinthian congregation was tearing itself apart. The Greek word translated as "divisions" in 1 Corinthians 1:10 is SKISMATA, from which we derive our English word *schisms*. There were schisms in Corinth. Paul describes them this way: "One of you says, 'I follow Paul;' another,

222

'I follow Apollos;' another, 'I follow Cephas;' still another, 'I follow Christ.' "

What were the Corinthians arguing about? Their favorite leaders. Not only this, but they were also suing each other in court, further tarnishing their reputation and the name of Christ. So we wonder: How could these Christians have acted this way toward one another? But then, this type of behavior is not exclusively Corinthian and it did not end in 58 A.D. Even the Lord's original twelve disciples argued over "who is the greatest in the kingdom of God."

Pride is the Cause of Divisiveness
Congregations may seem to split over silly things like carpet color, thermostat settings, the location of the piano, or the way a pastor shakes hands. But these are not the causes of division; they are the excuses. The real cause of divisiveness is human pride. The Greek word for "I" is EGO. And you can hear the EGO in the declarations: "I follow Paul. I follow Apollos." In other words, "My group is better than your group. I'm a better Christian than you are."

In Romans 12 Paul links harmonious living to the absence of pride, saying, "Live in harmony with one another. Do not be proud, but be willing to associate with people of low position. Do not be conceited." And in Romans 16 he reminds us that EGO is the true motive of false teachers and their divisive teaching. "For such people are not serving our Lord Christ, but their own appetites."

Jesus Christ is the Tie that Binds

If following selfish pursuits is the cause of divisiveness, what is the cure? Following Jesus Christ. What Jesus said to His first disciples He still says to us: "Follow Me." And when by God's grace we follow Jesus, by the very act of following we are all part of the same group. We are all going in the same direction. We are all keeping in step with each other.

Jesus Himself prayed for the unity of His followers, saying in John 17, "I pray also for those who will believe in Me through their message, that all of them may be one, Father, just as You are in Me and I am in You."

But this oneness is not based on an absence of truth, as far too many churches teach today: "Can't we call get along? Can't we put aside these doctrinal squabbles? It doesn't matter what you believe as long as you believe something. It doesn't matter which god you trust in as long as you trust in a god. It doesn't matter which scriptures you read—the Bible, the Koran, the Book of Mormon—as long as you read scripture. It doesn't matter how you're saved so long as you're saved." This is nonsense.

There is only one way to be saved, and it is through faith in Jesus Christ. And there is only one truth, and it is God's truth in His word; as Jesus said, "Sanctify them by the truth; Your word is truth," John 17:17.

THE VALUE OF MONEY

Mark 10:17-27

Money Can't Save

He was a man who had everything. Youth. Great wealth. A position of power. All the attributes the world craves. And yet, something critical was missing from this rich young ruler's life—something that his vast wealth could not obtain; namely, the certainty of eternal life, and with it, peace of heart and mind.

And so the rich man asked Jesus, "What shall I do to inherit eternal life?" This was not a casual question or a trick question, like those so often posed by the religious leaders of Israel. The rich man ran to Jesus. And when he asked his question, he did so on bended knees.

Startling, isn't it? This young man had everything, but was still unhappy and uncertain about his salvation. How many people are like him? How many have money in the bank but only emptiness in their hearts? Used wisely, money can accomplish wonderful things, but it can't save anyone from sin or purchase eternal life. Regardless of the size of the bank account, the spaciousness of the home, the make of the car, or the number of carats in the diamond—if we don't have Jesus Christ by faith, we have nothing of true value.

Works Can't Save

"What shall I do…?" the rich man asked. His assumption was that he could do something to inherit eternal life. This is always the assumption of human nature and always the teaching of manmade religions. But human works can never purchase salvation or bring peace of mind. Paul wrote to the Ephesians: "For it is by grace you have been saved, through faith—and this not from yourselves, it is the gift of God—not by works, so that no one can boast," Ephesians 2:8-9.

You and I know this lesson very well. But the rich young ruler didn't know it at all. This is why Jesus directed the man to the Ten Commandments, saying, "If you want to enter life, obey the commandments," Matthew 19:17. A serious appraisal of his life should have led the rich man to conclude that he could not keep God's commandments perfectly.

Yet, how did the rich man answer Jesus? "Teacher, all these things I have kept from my youth," Mark 10:20. Desiring to turn the man away from self-trust to trusting in God, Jesus lovingly gave him a commandment he was not able to keep. "One thing you lack," said Jesus. "Go your way, sell what you have and give it to the poor, and you will have treasure in heaven; and come, take up the cross, and follow Me," Mark 10:21. Rather than to part with his wealth, the rich man turned away from Christ.

Only God Can Save

Jesus neither commended nor condemned wealth. But He did warn against its limitations and dangers. "Children," He said, "how hard it is for those who trust in riches to enter the kingdom of God! It is easier for a camel to go through the eye of a needle than for a rich man to enter the kingdom of God," Mark 10:24-25.

At this, the disciples were greatly astonished. Why? Because if the rich can't earn their way to heaven, who can? If money can't buy forgiveness, what can? If human works can't obtain eternal life, what can?

Thankfully, God can and has through the suffering, death, and resurrection of His Son, Jesus Christ. As Jesus said, "With man this is impossible, but not with God; all things are possible with God," Mark 10:27.

WHEN FEELING DOWN

Psalm 42

The writer of Psalm 42 was depressed. He couldn't sleep or eat. He felt overwhelmed and isolated. He experienced severe mood changes. One minute he was jubilant, and the next moment despondent. He praised, then pleaded. He lauded God's faithfulness, then accused God of forgetfulness. Yet, amid his pain, he understood the way up and out of his depression.

When Feeling Down, Look Up

When feeling down, the psalmist looked up to God. "Put your hope in God," he told himself twice. We should tell ourselves the same in our moments of despair. Why is this so important? When depressed, our tendency is to look down instead of up, inward instead of outward. The more we look down, the more downward-looking we are. It is a vicious cycle.

This is why the psalmist directed himself and us to look up to God, "to the living God," Psalm 42:2—not to money, philosophy, affairs, illegal drugs or alcohol. These 'remedies' do not cure depression; they feed it.

God is the only Source of all hope, all power, and all encouragement; as Paul wrote: "Praise be to the God and Father of our Lord Jesus Christ, the Father of compassion and the God of all comfort, who comforts us in all our troubles," 2 Corinthians 1:3-4.

When Feeling Down, Speak Up

When feeling down, the psalmist prayed. "I pour out my soul," Psalm 42:4. In like manner, when we're depressed, we shouldn't keep the problem to ourselves. This merely increases the pain and isolation. Instead, we should speak up to God. For in giving our depression to Him, we experience that transcendent peace that only comes from presenting our needs to God.

Paul wrote in Philippians 4:6-7. "Do not be anxious about anything, but in everything, by prayer and petition, with thanksgiving, present your requests to God. And the peace of God, which transcends all understanding, will guard your hearts and your minds in Christ Jesus."

"Yes," we may say, "but I've prayed and prayed and I'm still depressed. God hasn't answered me." But are we truly listening? And even if the Almighty hasn't yet answered, He will. This is His promise. "Call upon Me in the day of trouble; I will deliver you, and you will honor Me," Psalm 50:15. Don't view prayer as merely therapeutic. View it as it truly is, powerful and effective.

When Feeling Down, Read Up

When feeling down, the psalmist undoubtedly read up on Scripture. The author of Psalm 130—another psalm about depression—wrote: "I wait for the LORD, my soul waits, and in His word I put my hope," Psalm 130:5.

Depression is often the result of how we think others see us or how we see ourselves. "I'm unattractive, undesirable, unwanted, and unloved." At all such times, it is vital that we realize how God sees us through Jesus Christ. He sees us as redeemed, restored, and forgiven; as born again and adopted into His family; as privileged to call Him "Abba"—Aramaic for "Daddy." And if God adopted us, then God wanted us. As we read the Scriptures, the reality of how God sees us will overcome the way we see ourselves.

When Feeling Down, Get Up

When feeling down, the psalmist desperately wanted to go to church. "When can I go and meet with God?" he asked in Psalm 42:2. And in verse 4 he wrote: "These things I remember as I pour out my soul: how I used to go with the multitude, leading the procession to the house of God, with shouts of joy and thanksgiving among the festive throng."

When depressed, we too need to get up and go to church, where we will hear the saving word of God and feel the love and support of fellow Christians. Staying away only feeds our depression instead of feeding our faith.

Conversely, when we look up to God, speak up in prayer, read up on Scripture, and get up and out to public worship—we should have every expectation that God will lift us out of our depression. We too should say with the psalmist: "For I will yet praise Him, my Savior and my God," Psalm 42:5,11.

WHEN GOD SAYS, "I LOVE YOU"

John 3:16

"I love you." Few phrases are more endearing and important. For human beings, however, love can have a variety of meanings—from the deep, committed love of husband and wife to the love of hamburgers, hotdogs, and blockbuster movies. And to make matters more complicated, we distinguish between types of love: parental love, marital love, romantic love, puppy love, Christian love, brotherly love, and friendship love.

What does God mean when He says "I love you"? While the answer is found throughout Scripture, nowhere is it more simply and eloquently stated than in John 3:16. "For God so loved the world that He gave His only begotten Son, that whoever believes in Him should not perish but have everlasting life."

The Greek word for love in this verse is AGAPE, the highest form of love. AGAPE-love is not based on feelings or emotions but on deep, factual commitment. It is a complete love, not lacking in any area or resource. It is a deliberate love, unwilling to give up or let go. It is a sacrificial love, willing to sacrifice itself in the interest of others. It is a purposeful love, focused on true need, not superficial want.

And most of all, AGAPE-love is a perfect love; so perfect, in fact, that this word is used to describe the perfect love of God the Father for God the Son in John 3:35, and later in John 14:31, the perfect love of God the Son for God the Father. This is God's perfect love for you, me, all of us.

"God so loved the world." But what kind of world? A world that deserved His love? No. A world that hated God and rejected the long-awaited Messiah—"slanderers, God-haters, insolent, arrogant, boastful, senseless, faithless, heartless, ruthless," Paul wrote in Romans 1:30.

This is the world God loved and for which He sacrificed His Son. God loves us for His own sake, for His own reasons. Can you think of anything more comforting? Being saved has nothing to do with social status or nice clothes or good deeds or large bank accounts. Being saved comes from trusting in Jesus Christ, the Savior whom God the Father sent as the fullest expression of His love.

Few things flow more easily from human lips than "I love you." But God didn't merely say "I love you." He proved His love eternally and irrevocably in a way that should eliminate all of our worries, fears, and doubts. He sacrificed His own Son.

If you find yourself worried or troubled today and want reassurance that God loves you, look at the cross of Jesus. And say with the apostle Paul in Romans 8: "What, then, shall we say in response to this? If God is for us, who can be against us? He who did not spare His own Son, but gave

232

Him up for us all—how will He not also, along with Him, graciously give us all things? Who shall separate us from the love of Christ? Shall trouble or hardship or persecution or famine or nakedness or danger or sword? No, in all these things we are more than conquerors through Him who loved us. For I am convinced that neither death nor life, neither angels nor demons, neither the present nor the future, nor any powers, neither height nor depth, nor anything else in all creation, will be able to separate us from the love of God that is in Christ Jesus our Lord."

WHEN HOPE LIES DEAD AND BURIED

John 11:17-27, 38-45

A Familiar Story

One day Lazarus was fine, out the door, and off to work. The next day he wasn't feeling well. A few days after that, he was gravely ill and dying; perhaps a man in his thirties, unmarried, and with a thousand unfulfilled dreams. Sound familiar? It should.

We've all lived versions of this story. And each version begins with a phrase like "Oh, I never expected that to happen." I never expected to lose my loved one. I never expected to live alone. I never expected to get sick. I never expected to go through a divorce." Don't you think Mary and Martha felt this way too? I do.

At times, difficult circumstances may be even worse for Christians—not because we doubt God's power, but because we confess it; not because we doubt God's love, but because we believe it.

When Lazarus became deathly ill, Mary and Martha sent Jesus a message. The message read, "Lord, the one You love is sick," John 11:3. They entrusted their brother to the love of Jesus. Yet, what must these sisters have thought as the hours became days, with no sign of Jesus? It's easy to imagine them at Lazarus' bedside; dabbing his feverish forehead with a cold, wet cloth; whispering to him, "Don't worry, Lazarus. Jesus is on the way. When He arrives, everything will be fine."

When the sisters were away from Lazarus, however, I wonder how often they stared out the window, shook their heads, and asked each other in hushed tones: "Where is Jesus? What's taking Him so long?"

John 11:5-6 states, "Jesus loved Martha and her sister and Lazarus. Yet, when He heard that Lazarus was sick, He stayed where He was two more days." How could Jesus love Lazarus, yet not go to his bedside immediately? Why not heal Lazarus long-distance? Jesus had the power.

God Deals with Us in Absolute Love

Ancient Greek had three primary words for love: EROS, meaning romantic love; PHILOS, meaning casual love or friendship; and AGAPE, the love of deep understanding and unswerving commitment.

When John 3:16 says that "God so loved the world," it uses the word AGAPE. When John 11:5 says that "Jesus loved Martha and her sister and Lazarus," it uses the word AGAPE. Clearly then, what Jesus did in delaying His trip to Bethany, as strange or troubling as this delay may seem, was done out of AGAPE; that deep, committed love. But there's more.

The word in John 11:6 often translated as "yet" is much more properly translated "therefore." When we make this substitution, notice what happens to the sense of these verses: "Jesus loved Martha and her sister and Lazarus. THEREFORE when He heard that Lazarus was sick, He stayed where He was two more days."

In other words, it was precisely because Jesus loved Martha, Mary, and Lazarus that He delayed going to Bethany. How vital that we remember this. God deals with us in the same way. We may not always understand the circumstances. We may not yet see the beautiful picture still lying in the jumble of puzzle pieces. But we can always be certain that God is dealing with us out of pure, absolute love.

God's Delays Have a Blessed Purpose

When God delays, He is inviting us to trust Him. He is teaching us patience. Learning patience is not easy in this world of immediate gratification, instant coffee, microwave dinners, and scratch-off lottery tickets.

Remaining patient is even more difficult when struggling with ongoing, unresolved problems. But through His delays, God in AGAPE is allowing something mighty, holy, and necessary to occur in our hearts and lives. By delaying, God allows time for the wrong kind of human hopes to grow ill, die, and be buried, while simultaneously leading us to put our hope in Him.

For Our Good and God's Glory

Though God may delay at times, the solution He will bring about will be for our good and His glory. Notice what Jesus says in John 11:4 about Lazarus' illness: "This sickness will not end in death. No, it is for God's glory so that God's Son may be glorified through it." In John 11:40 Jesus says to Martha: "Did I not tell you that if you believed, you would see the glory of God?"

I submit to you, Christian reader, that today and every day of our lives—especially during those dark days when all hope seems lost—God is saying exactly the same words to us: "Did I not tell you that if you believed, you would see the glory of God?" In Psalm 50 God invites, "Call upon Me in the day of trouble; I will deliver you, and you will glorify Me."

Have you ever considered that your "day of trouble" will not only result in you glorifying God, but also those who see your unshakable hope in God? It's true. John 12 tells us that many people believed in Jesus because of Lazarus.

Over my life, I've heard many people ask the question, "What's so important about hearing the word of God?" You'll find the answer written in John 11: "When He had said this, Jesus called out in a loud voice, 'Lazarus, come out!' The dead man came out, his hands and feet wrapped with strips of linen, and a cloth wrapped around his face."

Do we need more proof, more incentive, to hear God's word than this? When your hopes lie dead and buried, turn to the living word of God. Then do what the word of Christ empowered dead-and-buried Lazarus to do.

Take off your grave clothes and go free.

STRENGTH IN WEAKNESS

2 Corinthians 12:7-10

Humanly speaking, the apostle Paul had many reasons to boast. He was a called apostle of Jesus Christ "by the will of God," 2 Corinthians 12:1. He had demonstrated all the marks of a true apostle—"signs, wonders and miracles," 2 Corinthians 12:12. He had traveled farther, worked harder, and suffered more than many others, 2 Corinthians 11:21-27. He had been given surpassingly great "visions and revelations from the Lord," 2 Corinthians 12:1.

Yet, despite his many blessings and accomplishments, Paul desired only to boast of his weaknesses. "If I must boast," he said in 2 Corinthians 11:30, "I will boast of the things that show my weakness." Why? Because by God's grace, Paul had come to know the truthfulness of this paradox: "When I am weak, then I am strong," 2 Corinthians 12:7. One of the means through which Paul had learned this important lesson was a "thorn in the flesh."

Scholars have debated the nature of Paul's "thorn" for centuries. Theories have ranged from a particular temptation to illnesses like malaria, epilepsy, arthritis, and eye disease. While we don't know what Paul's thorn was, we do know why he received it. He tells us himself. "To keep me from becoming conceited because of these surpassingly great revelations, there was given me a thorn in the flesh, a messenger of Satan, to torment me," 2 Corinthians 12:7.

The Greek word for "to torment" is more literally "to go on beating with the fists." Whatever the thorn, it was a constant pain; a constant messenger of Paul's mortality and human weakness; and therein a constant reminder of the true source of wisdom and strength—God, not Paul.

We have thorns too, not always visible to others but still pestering and festering just below the surface of our daily lives. The thorns may be physical, financial, emotional, spiritual, or even the heartache caused by other people. As always, our first instinct is to ask God to take the thorn away. And sometimes He does.

At other times, however, God allows the thorn to remain, even though we can offer many sound reasons why the thorn is better out than in. "Lord, I would be so much happier if I could get out of debt. Lord, if I didn't have these health problems, I could spend more quality time with family members and help more at church. That's reasonable, isn't it, Lord?"

Yes, that's reasonable. But in God's redemptive care for our individual lives, what may be reasonable is not always beneficial. Three times Paul pleaded with God to remove his thorn. And he no doubt offered legitimate reasons too. "Lord, if you remove this burden, I will work even harder, travel even farther, reach even more people with the gospel of Christ." And God answered, No, Paul. "My grace is sufficient for you, for My power is made perfect in weakness," 2 Corinthians 12:9.

Understanding God's purpose in his life gave Paul a different perspective on thorns and problems, so that he could actually say, "Therefore I will boast all the more gladly about my weaknesses, so that Christ's power may rest on me. That is why, for Christ's sake, I delight in weaknesses, in insults, in hardships, in persecutions, in difficulties. For when I am weak, then I am strong."

Strength in weakness. There is not one aspect of the Christian life to which this wondrous paradox does not apply. Consider the matter of our eternal salvation. How are we saved? Are we saved by our own strength, or by admitting our dismal weakness and relying upon God's strength? Paul wrote to the Ephesians, "It is by grace you have been saved, through faith—and this not from yourselves; it is the gift of God—not by works, so that one one can boast," Ephesians 2:8-9.

I can think of nothing more comforting than the knowledge that God does the saving and we do the receving; that there is nothing we can do to save ourselves and nothing we need do other than to trust in our Lord and Savior, Jesus Christ.

What about prayer? When we face thorns and predicaments, our first resort is often to worry and our last resort is to pray. The first accomplishes nothing; the last accomplishes great things, as James wrote in his epistle: "Is any one of you in trouble? He should pray. The prayer of a righteous man is powerful and effective."

When we realize that we cannot solve all of our problems and instead commit them to the Lord—in that very instant our weakness is turned to God's strength. We are living the paradox "when I am weak, then I am strong."

David, who defeated Goliath. Abraham, whose body was reproductively dead. Moses, who complained, 'I can't speak.' Jeremiah, who worried, 'I am too young.' Elijah, who slumped beneath a juniper tree in despair. Peter, who denied knowing Christ. Paul, who pleaded with God to remove his thorn in the flesh. And even Jesus, who was crucified in what seemed to be frailty and weakness. All of these and more, including your life and mine, are shining examples of God's power made perfect in weakness.

WHO'S IN CHARGE HERE ANYWAY?

1 Corinthians 15:20-28

So much of today's news is bad news: wars, terrorism, natural disasters, economic distress, senseless crimes, and deadly, contagious diseases. When we look at the headlines, we may wonder, "Who's in charge here anyway?"

We may ask the same question about the Christian community. Jesus said in Matthew 16: "On this rock"—that is, Peter's confession of Jesus as Lord and Christ—"I will build My church, and the gates of Hades will not overcome it." And yet, how small, helpless, and insignificant the Christian community often seems when compared to the collective voices and forces of its many foes.

Or what of your personal life? Do the circumstances of your life appear chaotic and out of control? Are you asking, "Who's in charge here anyway?"

The Bible repeatedly assures us that Jesus Christ is in control of all things: the world, the church, and our individual lives. Paul wrote to the Corinthians, "For He must reign until He has put all His enemies under His feet." He told the Romans, "Christ, who is God over all." He reminded the Colossians that Christ created all things, rules all things, and holds all things together, "so that in everything He might have the supremacy."

And this Jesus is not only our almighty King, He's our all-caring King; the King who willingly wore a crown of thorns and endured the spitting, beating, and mockery of Roman soldiers. How important that we see Jesus in these two ways—almighty in power and eternal in compassion, ruling the universe and ruling in our hearts—as we face the challenges and difficulties of our lives.

The next time you watch the Six O'clock News and see angry terrorists raising their fists and shouting "death to America," remember: Terrorists are not in charge here. Jesus Christ is. The next time you hear worrisome phrases like "global recession" or "super inflation," remember: The Federal Reserve Board and Wall Street are not in charge here. Jesus Christ is. The next time you grow dismayed by the small size of your congregation and wonder how you will carry out a gospel ministry, remember: You are not in charge of your congregation. Jesus Christ is.

You, dear Christian friend, are not the victim of fate or circumstances. You are a redeemed subject of the King of Kings.

WHO IS THE GREATEST?

Mark 9:30-37

The world invariably defines greatness by what one has and does. But in the kingdom of God definitions are very different.

In God's Kingdom, Greatness is Selflessness

Jesus said, "If anyone wants to be first, he must be the very last," Mark 9:35. This statement makes no sense to a world which views first as greatest and last as regrettable. Yet, Jesus insisted that putting others first and self last is greatness in the kingdom of God.

In God's kingdom greatness is not climbing the ladder to success, but rather holding the ladder while others climb too. And why should Christians want to be selfless? Because their Savior was selfless, as Paul explained in Philippians 2:5-7, "Your attitude should be the same as that of Christ Jesus: Who, being in very nature God, did not consider equality with God something to be grasped, but made Himself nothing, taking the very nature of a servant, being made in human likeness."

In God's Kingdom, Greatness is Service

Jesus also said, "If anyone wants to be first, he must be... the servant of all," Mark 9:35. The Greek word for servant in this verse, DIAKONOS, is the source of our English term "deacon;" a servant, attendant, or minister. Etymologically,

244

DIAKONOS is from two other Greek words, which together can mean order-taker or errand-runner. Imagine using such terms in a help wanted ad. Even in today's difficult economy, how much interest would words like errand-runner or order-taker generate?

In the kingdom of men it is not the servant who is great, but the person who has a great servant.

But this is not the case in the kingdom of God. Jesus taught His disciples, "You know that those who are regarded as rulers of the Gentiles lord it over them, and their high officials exercise authority over them. Not so with you. Instead, whoever wants to become great among you must be your servant, and whoever wants to be first must be slave of all. For even the Son of Man did not come to be served, but to give His life as a ransom for many," Mark 10:42-45

In God's Kingdom, Greatness is Humility

The word "humble" does not appear in our text. However, humility is implied by the small child Jesus set before His bickering disciples. And the word humble is used in the parallel account of Matthew 18:4, where Jesus said, "Therefore, whoever humbles himself like this child is the greatest in the kingdom of heaven."

Clearly, we won't find this advice in college curriculums or motivational lectures or assertiveness trainings. The world does not view humility as an asset, but as a liability. In the world's view it is not the meek and humble who will inherit the earth, but the strong and relentless; the people who will do whatever it takes to achieve personal greatness.

But to the Most High God, humility is of great worth. As the Psalmist wrote, "The sacrifices of God are a broken spirit; a broken and contrite heart, O God, You will not despise," Psalm 51:17. To see the greatest example of humility, we need only look to Jesus Christ, of whom Paul wrote in Philippians 2: "And being found in appearance as a man, He humbled Himself and became obedient to death— even death on a cross."

In God's Kingdom, Greatness is Childlike Faith

That small child Jesus placed before His disciples not only exemplified great humility but also great faith— childlike faith. In the kingdom of men children are often shushed and pushed aside as of no significance. Even the Lord's disciples tried to prevent little children from approaching Jesus.

But when Jesus saw this, He was indignant, saying, "Let the little children come to Me, and do not hinder them, for the kingdom of God belongs to such as these. I tell you the truth, anyone who will not receive the kingdom of God like a little child will never enter it," Mark 10:14-15.

In God's kingdom the faith that embraces, trusts, follows, and clings to God like a little child is a great faith.

WHY, GOD?

1 Peter 1:3-9

The Origin of Trials

Contrary to popular belief, God is not the cause of every problem in our lives; though we are often quick to blame Him. Yes, God is the Sovereign Ruler of the universe. Nothing can happen without His direction or permission. However, God is never the origin of evil. The apostle James wrote, "When tempted, no one should say, 'God is tempting me.' For God cannot be tempted by evil, nor does He tempt anyone," James 1:13.

Our world is filled with untold suffering, sickness, and death. But is this the world God created or desired for us? No. Therefore, before we accuse Him of causing all miseries and ills, let's read the reality of Romans 5:12, "Therefore, just as sin entered the world through one man, and death through sin, and in this way death came to all men, because all sinned."

At times, we bring trials and troubles into our lives. If I smoke cigarettes for thirty years and get lung cancer, is God to blame or am I? If I abuse alcohol for decades and develop cirrhosis of the liver, is God to blame or am I? If I am unfaithful to my spouse and my marriage fails, is God to blame or am I? In such cases I should not be asking "Why, God?" but rather "Why did I do this to myself?"

Does God send or allow trials in our lives? Of course. But when He does, He always assures us of three things. First, whatever the trouble, nothing can rob us of our eternal salvation or separate us from God's redemptive love in Jesus Christ. We have an inheritance that "can never perish, spoil or fade," 1 Peter 1:4.

Second, every trial is under God's complete control, as Paul explained in 1 Corinthians 10:13, "God is faithful; He will not let you be tempted beyond what you can bear. But when you are tempted, He will also provide a way out so that you can stand up under it." God knows exactly what to send into our lives, exactly when to send it, exactly when to end it, and exactly what He wants to accomplish through it.

And third, every trial in a Christian's life has a divine purpose. That purpose is not to harm, but to heal; not to destroy, but to save; not to do something bad to us, but to do something blessed for us.

The Purpose of Trials

Trials strengthen faith. Biologically, it is impossible to build muscle up without tearing it down. How is this often done? By lifting weights in a gymnasium. And what is true biologically is true spiritually.

For faith to grow up and grow strong, it must exercise regularly and stay on a steady diet of God's Word. Yet, who among us would exercise our own faith? Do we even regularly exercise our bodies? This is why God exercises our faith for us. And how does He do it? Often through weights, heavy burdens, and persistent problems.

The most important thing in our lives is not our jobs, bank accounts, family heirlooms, homes, recreation, health, or even loved ones. The most important thing is our faith in Jesus Christ, because through it God saves us.

And this is why the Almighty does whatever He needs to do to strengthen our faith and make it genuine. As Peter wrote, speaking expressly of trials: "These have come so that your faith—of greater worth than gold, which perishes even though refined by fire—may be proved genuine and may result in praise, glory and honor when Jesus Christ is revealed," 1 Peter 1:7.

Trials reveal our weaknesses and teach us to rely on God's strength. Another word for "trial" is "test." What is the purpose of a school test? To reveal what a student has learned, as well as areas needing improvement. Tests are not designed to make students fail, but to help them improve and succeed. And the same is true of the tests and trials God allows in our lives.

Remember Paul's "thorn in the flesh," whatever it may have been—recurring malaria or an eye disease? Can't you imagine Paul asking "Why, God? This problem is hindering my ministry. Take it away. Please." But God replied, "My grace is sufficient for you, for My power is made perfect in weakness," 2 Corinthians 12:3.

Trials teach us what is truly important in life. The hymnist has written: "When every earthly prop gives way, He then is all my Hope and Stay. On Christ, the solid Rock I stand. All other ground is sinking sand."

This is the reality: You and I are never more mindful of God, never feel more of a need for God, than when we endure trials. All of us know this to be true. So, if today we find ourselves neglecting God or wandering away from God, should we not expect God to allow some trial into our lives? And when He does, should we not drop to our knees and thank Him for His love and faithfulness?

At times, one trial may prevent a far worse trial. On the day before my son Andrew and I moved to Florida, my car overheated while we were running errands. I was furious. "Why, God?" I asked. "This is all I need. I have so much to do." The problem turned out to be a cracked radiator hose.

On my way home from the auto repair shop, I realized something important. Had my car not overheated when and where it did—it could have happened during the long drive to Florida, along some deserted stretch of two-lane blacktop, where cell phone coverage was poor and repair shops were nonexistent. God used one small problem to prevent a much larger one.

Trials are often a form of much-needed discipline. Parents, did you discipline your children? Why? To make their lives painful and miserable? Of course not. You disciplined them because you wanted to make their lives better; because you wanted to keep them safe, and to teach them right from wrong; and all because you love them.

God disciplines us for the same reason; namely, He loves us. As explained in Hebrews 12: " 'My son, do not make light of the Lord's discipline, and do not lose heart when He rebukes you, because the Lord disciplines those He loves, and He punishes everyone He accepts as a son.' Endure hardship as discipline. God is treating you as sons."

Trials and troubles are never easy. But remember: Even if you cannot always trace the movement of God's hand, you can always rely on the proven love in His heart.

WITNESSES FOR CHRIST

John 1:29-41

Witnesses for Christ. What a wonderful phrase! What a remarkable privilege! Yet, few things make Christians more uneasy than witnessing. At times, the very thought of sharing Christ with a stranger, friend, or even a loved one can fill us with dread. We may be tempted to look for every 'reasonable' excuse not to witness: "Oh, I'm not qualified. I have no training or materials. Witnessing is the pastor's job."

For all our worry about logistics, tactics, and materials (important things, perhaps, but not the most important things), we make witnessing for Christ far more complicated than it is. Witnessing is not a professional process. It is a *personal* process. It does not start with our witness to others but God's witness to us.

God's Witness to John the Baptist

John the Baptist and Jesus were cousins. John knew who Jesus was. He knew that Jesus was the Messiah. So did John's mother Elizabeth, who said to the Virgin Mary, "Why am I so favored, that the mother of my Lord should come to me?" John's father, Zechariah, prophesied of his son, "And you, my child, will be called a prophet of the Most High; for you will go on before the Lord to prepare the way for Him."

Who can doubt that John discussed these things with his parents many times over the years? And John certainly recognized Jesus as the Messiah when Jesus came to him for baptism. John tried to deter Jesus, saying, "I need to be baptized by You, and do You come to me?"

Yet, twice in John 1:29-41, John the Baptist says of Jesus, "I did not know Him." What is he telling us? That he did not recognize his own cousin? No. He's telling us that based on outward appearances he would not have recognized Jesus as the Messiah.

Jesus was poor. Jesus was ordinary-looking. By His own admission, Jesus had no place to call home. On his own, John the Baptist would have never recognized Jesus as the Messiah. He did not point others to Christ; he did not witness about Christ; he did not specifically say "Jesus Christ is the Lamb of God who takes away the sin of the world"—*until* God the Father revealed this to him by means of the Holy Spirit descending upon Jesus like a dove.

God's Witness to Us

The same is true of us. We were not eyewitnesses of Christ's glory; but God has nevertheless revealed that glory to us. We did not see the Holy Spirit descending upon Jesus like a dove; but in a real sense the Holy Spirit has descended upon us, empowering us to believe that the poor, ordinary-looking Jesus of Nazareth is the Son of God and Savior of the world. We did not hear God the Father say at Christ's baptism, "This is My Son, whom I love; with Him

I am well pleased;" but we hear the very same words of the same heavenly Father in the pages of Scripture.

What great truths God has revealed to us in His word! We know that God created us. We know what's wrong with this world—sin. We know that we are not saved by doing, but by believing in Jesus Christ. We know the miracles of Jesus recorded in Scripture, and of equal importance, why He performed miracles. By God's grace and power, we've come to see what no human eyes can see apart from the Holy Spirit; namely, that Jesus Christ is the Lamb of God who takes away the sin of the world.

Witnessing to What We've Witnessed

Most of us can't wait to tell others about persons, places, or events we've seen. "Oh, you'll never guess what I saw today!" A famous celebrity. A well-known politician. A rock star. An automobile accident. Mickey Mouse. A million dollar home in the country. An NFL quarterback.

By God's grace, we've come to see Jesus Christ as our Lord and Savior; the one who willingly suffered, died, and rose again for all of us. With the apostle John, we can say, "The Word became flesh and made His dwelling among us. We have seen His glory, the glory of the One and Only Son, who came from the Father, full of grace and truth."

Isn't that worth talking about?

YOU HAVE A CALL FROM JESUS

Mark 1:14-20

In 1975 the group Manhattan Transfer recorded a song titled *Operator*. In part the lyrics went: "Operator, information, give me Jesus on the line. Operator, information, I'd like to speak to a friend of mine." By some strange association—perhaps a connection between "Jesus on the line" and the "call" of the first disciples—I began to hear the lyrics of this song while studying Mark 1:14-20. I wondered, "So, what would I do if Jesus really did call me by phone? Would I rejoice in the opportunity to hear His voice or, depending on how busy I was, let the Savior go to voicemail?

A Call Through the Word

You really do have a call from Jesus; not a phone call, but a call to discipleship like Peter and Andrew, James and John. "Come, follow Me," Jesus said to those first disciples. And He calls us in the same way; namely, through His word.

The word of Jesus moved simple fishermen to leave everything in order to follow Him, even when they had no idea where He was leading. Amazing? Yes, but no more amazing than Paul saying, "I am not ashamed of the gospel, because it is the power of God for the salvation of everyone who believes," Romans 1:16. When you feel lost, alone, depressed, hurting, overwhelmed by sin and guilt, where should you turn? Shouldn't it be to the word of Christ?

A Personal Call

Years ago, many well-intentioned Christians wore buttons proclaiming "I Found It," referring to salvation in Christ. But is this really how discipleship works? Throughout Mark 1:14-20, Jesus is the one who is searching, finding, calling, and saving.

In the same way, it is Jesus who found, called, and saved you. "You did not choose Me," Jesus said in John 15:16, "but I chose you." If Jesus sought you, will He forsake you? If Jesus called you, will you ever receive a poor connection or busy signal when you call upon Him? Not a chance.

An Urgent Call

A sense of urgency pervades Mark 1:14-20. The Greek word translated "proclaiming" in verse 14 means to cry out with a loud voice. In verse 15 Jesus declares, "The time has come. The kingdom of God is near." The nearness of the kingdom underscores the urgency to enter it. According to verse 18, Peter and Andrew left their nets "at once" to follow Jesus. Verse 20 states that "without delay" Jesus called James and John.

Scripture never describes following Christ in terms of yesterday or tomorrow but always today. "Today, if you hear His voice, do not harden your hearts," Hebrews 4:7. Will any human being be able to stand before the judgment seat of Christ and explain away rejecting Christ by saying, "I'm sorry, Lord, but I didn't have time or opportunity to heed Your call?" Now is the time. Today is the day.

A Call to Change

"Repent and believe," Jesus said. Repentance is often associated with sorrow over sin and turning to God for forgiveness. This is absolutely true. But the New Testament word for repentance—METANOIA in Greek—literally means 'to change one's mind.' Change one's mind about what? Everything. Choices. Priorities. Language. Relationships. Behavior. The means to salvation; specifically, the understanding that as sinful human beings we cannot save ourselves. Our salvation comes entirely from God. We can't follow Jesus and still go in a different direction. "Follow Me," He said.

A Call to Service

By His call Jesus empowered average, unschooled fishermen to become fishers of men. Through their writings and ministries, the good news of Jesus Christ spread throughout the ancient world, and in the space of three centuries conquered the pagan Roman empire that had lasted for a thousand years.

You and I are not called to be apostles. However, Jesus does call each of us to serve Him in His kingdom. Whatever our form of service, whether pastor or teacher, organist or acolyte, doctor or plumber, husband or wife, mother or father—whatever Christ calls us to do, Christ will empower us to do. "I will make you fishers of men," He said.

You have a call from Jesus. Is that the phone ringing? Could you answer it?

CASE NUMBER J81-11

John 8:1-11

I've come to think of it as Case Number J81-11, that is, John 8:1-11; the account of a woman caught in the act of adultery; rushed from the bedroom to the courtroom by religious authorities; and condemned to death. In reality, as frightened and distraught as the woman was, she may have been only incidental to the case—merely used by the plaintiffs, the scribes and Pharisees, to find a basis to discredit Jesus.

Under the Mosaic Law, both the adulterer and adulteress were to be put to death. Yet, in Case Number J81-11, only the adulteress was present in court. How could this be when she was caught in the very act of adultery? Where was the man who was caught in the same act? Some believe that the man himself was part of the plot. Once his part was accomplished, he was set free.

If true, consider the implications. Consider that the holier-than-thou religious leaders in Jerusalem may have orchestrated an act of adultery simply to ensnare Jesus. They told Jesus, "In the Law Moses commanded us to stone such women. Now what do You think?" As John explained, "They were using this question as a trap, in order to have a basis to accuse Him," John 8:5-6.

What did Jesus do? He ignored them. Instead of answering, He stooped down and wrote on the ground. When the plaintiffs persisted in questioning Him, He stood, spoke a single sentence, knelt down again, and continued writing. This is what Jesus said: "If any one of you is without sin, let him be the first to throw a stone at her," John 8:7. "At this, those who heard began to go away one at a time, the older ones first, until only Jesus was left, with the woman still standing there," John 8:9.

And then the most touching scene of all; a scene I can barely read without feeling a swell of emotion. Jesus Christ, the Son of God—the only one in court that day who had a right to throw a stone—instead, offered the condemned woman love, mercy, and forgiveness; a woman who had been crushed by the reality of her sin and the enormity of her guilt. "Woman," asked Jesus, "where are they? Has no one condemned you?" She answered, "No one, sir." And Jesus said, "Then neither do I condemn you. Go now and leave your life of sin," John 8:10-12.

Why does this case, Case Number J81-11, so comfort and inspire us? Is it simply that the self-righteous scribes and Pharisees failed in their plot to discredit Jesus; or that the accusers in the crowd dropped the case and rocks and walked away? Is it simply the vivid image of the woman caught in the act of adultery—ashamed, embarrassed, bereft of dignity and hope, perhaps cringing on the ground with tears streaking the dust on her face? These are all important aspects of the case, but not the most important aspect.

No, the most important aspect of Case Number J81-11 is this: We have all been like that woman. We have all been "caught in the act" of sinning against God. And we have all been shown the undeserved love, mercy, and forgiveness of God in Jesus Christ.

If we do not see ourselves as sinful, then we do not understand the law of God any better than the scribes and Pharisees; and they were the legal experts. And if we insist on throwing stones at contrite sinners, who have repented of their sins and asked for forgiveness; then we do not understand the gospel of God either—or how much we ourselves have been forgiven.

FROM BABEL-ING TO BLENDING

Acts 2:5-12

When President Carter traveled to Poland in 1979, the U.S. State Department hired a Russian interpreter to translate his speeches. Unfortunately, while the interpreter understood Polish, he was not skilled at diplomacy. Consequently, Carter's "I left America" became "I abandoned America;" and his reference to "your desires for the future" became "your lusts for the future." The U.S and Poland had a good laugh.

The confusion of language is the direct result of the Tower of Babel. After the Flood, God commanded Noah and his sons to "be fruitful and increase in number and fill the earth," Genesis 9:1. Noah's descendants, however, chose to remain in one place, glorifying themselves instead of glorifying God. "Come," they said, "let us build ourselves a city, with a tower that reaches to the heavens, so that we may make a name for ourselves and not be scattered over the face of the whole earth," Genesis 11:4. These people were able to live together, work together, and scheme together because they spoke the same language.

God's response was to confuse the world's language at Babel, forcing mankind to separate into linguistic groups. Imagine how those city-planners and tower-builders felt when they were suddenly unable to communicate. They grew angry, frustrated, and suspicious. They threw up their hands and threw down their chisels and went their separate ways.

In a sense, Pentecost was the opposite of Babel. At Babel, many languages led to many nations and cultures; but at Pentecost, many languages led to one people of God from every nation. Babel was about separating; Pentecost about gathering. Babel, disunity; Pentecost, unity. What then may we learn about the outpouring of the Holy Spirit on Pentecost; how He leads us from confusion to clarity, from unbelief to faith, from Babel-ing to blending?

The Holy Spirit does the Work

Everything that happened on the First Pentecost, from the miracle of languages, to the miracle of faith, to the miraculous birth of the New Testament Church, was due solely to the work of the Holy Spirit. Through the Holy Spirit, simple Galilean fishermen were empowered to proclaim the "wonders of God" in languages they had not learned. Through the Spirit, three thousand came to faith in Jesus in one day.

The same is true of us. We did not come to Christ on our own. The Holy Spirit led us to Christ. We did not believe in Jesus on our own. The Holy Spirit created faith in our hearts, fanning it into flames as He did the tongues of fire on the day of Pentecost. We did not "see the light" on our own. The Holy Spirit illuminated us by the gospel.

The Holy Spirit Uses Means

The Spirit of God works through the very Scriptures He inspired. This is an important lesson for the Christian Church in every age and every place—and one we easily forget. As a pastor, I forget this lesson when I think that creating and sustaining faith has anything to do with the eloquence of my speech or the inflections of my voice or the outlines of my sermons.

As Christian congregations, we forget this lesson when we think our success depends on massive budgets, ideal locations, and state-of-the-art equipment. On the First Pentecost, Peter and the other apostles preached God's word, but *they* led no one to faith. Rather, according to Acts 2:47, "And the Lord added to their number daily those who were being saved." Who? The Lord, not us.

The Holy Spirit Brings Unity

Surely unity is the exact opposite of the separation and confusion at the Tower of Babel. This unity is based on faith in Christ; on the conviction of sins and confession of grace, as Paul stated in Romans 3:22-24, "There is no difference, for all have sinned and fall short of the glory of God, being justified freely by His grace through the redemption that is in Christ Jesus."

Imagine how startling and uplifting it was for people of the First Century A.D.—a society of wide divergence, rich and poor, free and slave, male and female; a society where women were often considered no more than property—to hear the proclamation: "There is neither Jew nor Greek, there is neither slave nor free, there is neither male nor female; for you are all one in Christ Jesus," Galatians 3:28.